Writers' Retreats

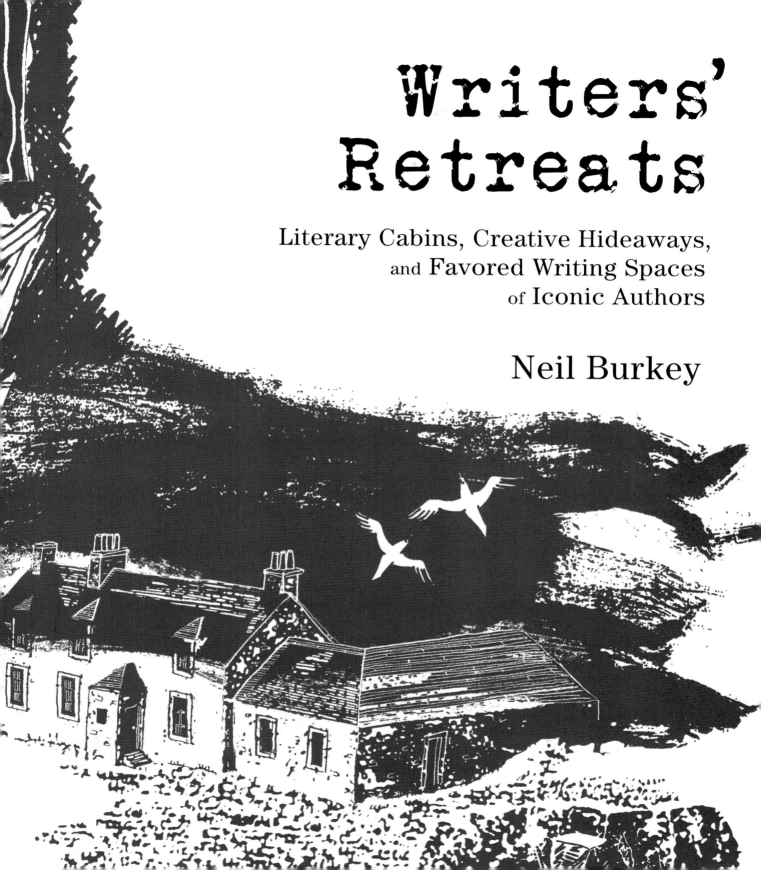

Writers' Retreats

Literary Cabins, Creative Hideaways, and Favored Writing Spaces of Iconic Authors

Neil Burkey

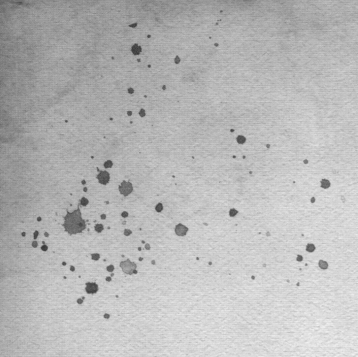

An Imagine Book
Published by Charlesbridge
9 Galen Street
Watertown, MA 02472
(617) 926-0329
www.imaginebooks.net

Editorial director: Will Steeds
Copyeditor: Andrew Lowe
Book design: Paul Palmer-Edwards
Illustrator: Robert Littleford

Library of Congress Cataloging-in-Publication Data

Names: Burkey, Neil, author.

Title: Writers' retreats : literary cabins, creative hideaways, and
favorite writing spaces of iconic authors / by Neil Burkey.

Description: Watertown, MA : Charlesbridge Publishing, [2021] |
Includes bibliographical references and index. | Summary: "An
exploration of the quirky, private, and sometimes curious places where
great writers work, unveiling the stories associated with them and the
literature that was conceived and written in them. With specially
commissioned illustrations" — Provided by publisher.

Identifiers: LCCN 2020056739 (print) | LCCN 2020056740 (ebook)
ISBN 9781623545109 (hardcover) | ISBN 9781632892348 (ebook)

Subjects: LCSH: Literary landmarks.

Classification: LCC PN164 .B87 2021 (print) | LCC PN164 (ebook) |
DDC 809--dc23
LC record available at https://lccn.loc.gov/2020056739
LC ebook record available at https://lccn.loc.gov/2020056740

Printed in China
(hc) 10 9 8 7 6 5 4 3 2 1

> "... imagine a room, like many thousands, with a window looking across people's hats and vans and motor-cars to other windows, and on the table inside the room a blank sheet of paper ..."
>
> —**Virginia Woolf**

Accordingly, the mood of each entry is written to match its moment, be it lighthearted or fraught, contented or imperiled, tragic or triumphant. As brevity necessitates compression, the book generally neglects each author's life beyond the moment represented. Ten of the entries are double-length, giving the authors a bit more elbow room, a bit more space to prop their writing tables. Wedged into each section is a special feature looking at other ways that writers retreat: behind a pseudonym, within a collective, away on a residency, into academia, amidst ritual, or, less happily, behind bars.

A retreat means different things to different writers at different times. For established, successful writers, or ones with the benefit of wealth, it might be an extra room in the house or a shed in the garden—perhaps especially built for that purpose. A place to find some peace while you knit your tapestry of words. Walls and a door to put you at a remove from external disturbances such as children or journalists. For others it might be a literal escape from persecution—or from the threat of death. It can also be more of a concept than a single location. A hotel room. A region. A movable feast.

Some authors are born with writers' retreats, some achieve writers' retreats, and others have writers' retreats thrust upon them. It's all down to class, political context, gumption, luck, and, of course, greatness. It's what they do with their writers' retreats that matters.

How does place correspond with inspiration? When does location equal creation? Can the view from a window change an author's interior perspective? What seeps in? Can a house make a writer? Can it unmake a writer? Does it matter where a writer writes? Let's see if we can find out.

Neil Burkey

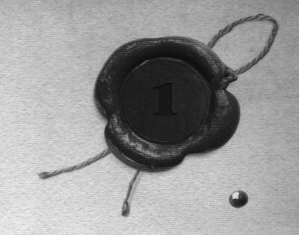

Home
from Home

Emily Dickinson

Born: December 10, 1830, Amherst, Massachusetts
Died: May 15, 1886, Amherst, Massachusetts

Bedroom, the Homestead, Amherst, Massachusetts

From the cherry writing table in the southwest corner of Dickinson's bedroom she could see Mount Holyoke Range and hear the voices of people passing by in the street below. She wrote nearly all of her roughly 1,800 poems at this table, along with the thousands of letters that increasingly served as her only connection with the outside world.

"I took one Draught of Life -
I'll tell you what I paid -
Precisely an existence -
The market price, they said."

—Emily Dickinson

Perhaps more than any other writer, Emily Dickinson had a creative life intertwined with her house. She was born there, and she died there, essentially unknown outside her immediate circle of acquaintances. Since that time, she has come to be recognized not only as one of the greatest poets ever to lay pen to paper, but also as one of literary history's most reclusive figures.

The Homestead is a broad-shouldered, symmetrical, two-story house built by Dickinson's grandfather in 1813, one of the first in Amherst to be made from bricks. Dickinson lived there until she was nine, when her father, Edward (a prominent lawyer and future congressman), moved the family to a home overlooking a cemetery on Pleasant Street, a mile away. Dickinson was twenty-four when the family moved back to the Homestead; it was to be her last move. She was not initially keen on the homecoming, as is reflected in a series of somber poems she wrote on the theme soon after, such as one with the initial line "I know some lonely Houses off the Road," or another that begins:

> There's been a Death, in the Opposite House,
> As lately as Today –
> I know it, by the numb look
> Such Houses have – alway –

But she adapted, and soon could scarcely imagine living anywhere else. The situation was improved further when her father built a home a stone's throw away called the Evergreens for his son Austin (whom Dickinson adored) and Austin's wife, Susan Huntington Gilbert, perhaps Dickinson's closest companion.

Although Dickinson's first forays into poetry occurred during her teenage years, she wasn't to find her true stride as an artist until her late twenties, experiencing an intense period of creativity shortly after moving into the Homestead, between 1858 and 1865 (roughly overlapping with the Civil War). Despite the fact that Dickinson's retiring nature prevented her from venturing far from home, her intellectual heft and emotional perspicuity bound her significantly to the world around her, eventually giving her a radius of influence that vastly outstripped her footfall.

The Homestead provided fodder for Dickinson's great allegorical devices, and the bones of architecture abound in her poetry—doors, hinges, beams, windows. There was the mausoleum-like salon, with its mahogany and marble and movable walls, creating new, impermanent spaces, shifting from public to private and back again, where Dickinson, always attuned to a dramatic gesture, could play the piano unseen by visitors.

> I am alive – because
> I am not in a Room –
> The Parlor – Commonly – it is –
> So Visitors may come –
>
> And lean – and view it sidewise –
> And add "How cold – it grew" –
> And "Was it conscious – when it stepped
> In Immortality?"
>
> I am alive – because
> I do not own a House –
> Entitled to myself – precise –
> And fitting no one else –
>
> And marked my Girlhood's name –
> So Visitors may know
> Which Door is mine – and not mistake –
> And try another Key –

▲ Facsimile reprint of the first edition of Emily Dickinson's *Poems*, published by Roberts Brothers in 1890. The flower is the "ghost" plant or "Indian pipe," *Monotropa uniflora*— possibly chosen because Dickinson's friend and editor, Mabel Loomis Todd, sent her a botanical painting of the plant. Dickinson was keenly interested in flowers and gardening, and called the Indian pipe "the preferred flower of life."

Indeed, the Dickinson home was a hub of activity, as her father's law office was only a few blocks away. This proximity resulted in frequent meetings and dinners being held at the house for the local cultural elite drawn by Edward and, later, Austin, after he had followed his father into the business. It was common for visitors to stop by the house to make a request or pay a courtesy. (In a letter, Dickinson described herself as having "eyes like the sherry in the glass that the guest leaves.")

Dickinson's bedroom served as a respite from this surplus of social obligation, facilitated by renovations carried out when the Dickinsons returned to the Homestead, including installation of cast-iron fireplaces in all of the main rooms (including Emily's bedroom). This meant that the family no longer needed to gravitate around a single open fire. Such innovations offered the Dickinsons the option of respite from one another as well.

The bedroom, fifteen square feet with a ten-foot ceiling and two large south-facing windows, was anything but claustrophobic. Its white walls and straw mats added to the room's airy aspect, as did the white linen bedsheets on her small sleigh-shaped mahogany bed. On the walls were portraits of George Eliot, Elizabeth Barrett Browning, and Thomas Carlyle.

> "To live is so startling, it leaves but little
> room for other occupations."
>
> —Emily Dickinson

Another key private space could be found in the small cupola at the top of the house, with panoptic views. It was accessed by climbing a spiral staircase outside Dickinson's bedroom, then traversing an unused attic space, a remove and vantage point that lent the six-foot-square room the austere serenity of a chapel.

> I dwell in Possibility –
> A fairer House than Prose –
> More numerous of Windows – Superior –
> for Doors –

Dickinson also kept a flower garden, rich with sweet peas, marigolds, lilies, and pansies. She would often send cuttings to friends, bundled with poems. Her father later added a conservatory to the property, where Emily could continue to garden all year round.

Although Dickinson is often presented as being withdrawn from society, she also here had dominion over it, and a fine perspective. Dickinson's sparse poetry favored structure (or "Circumference") over decoration, having "no room for petty furniture." Or, as she put it in one of her most economical poems,

> All things swept sole away
> This – is immensity –

She was acutely aware of her spatial surroundings, listening to the voices of visitors from a darkened hallway, lowering a basket of gingerbread from her bedroom window, talking with guests behind a closed door. And she had a love of solitude, quietly rebelling against the presiding culture, enjoying a radical interior life, rejecting a standard external life. Throughout her self-imposed self-incarceration, within her "Mansion of the Universe," she breathed life to spatial metaphors that formed the concepts of mortality, despair, and joy.

The handful of her poems that were published, in newspapers, were printed anonymously and apparently without her consent, and the vast majority of her work remained known only to its author. In 1865, Dickinson traveled to Boston for treatment for an eye condition, after which she never left Amherst again, rarely straying beyond the flowered grounds of the Homestead.

Marilynne Robinson

Born: November 26, 1943, Sandpoint, Idaho

The Middle West, Iowa City, Iowa

Having grown up in Idaho, Robinson has been attuned to the machinations and desires of people in rural towns. She is also a dedicated Calvinist, and while in Iowa occasionally gave sermons at her local Congregationalist church. As a writer, she sees it as her duty to do no harm, realizing that this belief may set her apart from many of her contemporaries.

> ## "Memory can make a thing seem to have been much more than it was."
>
> —Marilynne Robinson

In 1990, when the director of the Iowa Writers' Workshop offered Marilynne Robinson a position as professor, she declined. A year later she received a message from an administrator with the program—via telegram. This caught her attention; she didn't know anyone sent telegrams anymore. It was enough to convince her to accept the invitation, agreeing to teach for two years. She remained in the position for a quarter century.

Robinson had never expected to live in the Middle West (a usage she came to prefer over "Midwest"), as she had harbored the usual prejudices about the region. And she couldn't live in a place without knowing its history—but when she arrived in Iowa, she was told that it had no history. Knowing this was nonsense, she began reading everything she could find, discovering abolitionist origins, antebellum integrated schools, and an abundance of other examples demonstrating the region's liberal past.

Her research formed the basis of the creation of Gilead, the fictional Middle West town where all of Robinson's novels from that point on have been set. Having not published a novel since her 1980 debut, *Housekeeping*, she now had found her Yoknapatawpha—though it would be more than a decade before she started writing about it. After finishing *Gilead* (2004), she missed her characters, and so she returned to them, again and again.

She worried at first that teaching would compromise her creative energies, but she soon found that teaching, apart from being a distraction and a burden, could also be a catalyst for writing. And she didn't teach technique at the Workshop, as she found that most technical problems dissolved once a writer realized where the life of a story lay. Also, the social life of the Iowa Workshop gradually shifted away from its earlier, more raucous incarnations, until it was mostly the quietest among the faculty who remained, happy to keep to themselves—leaving Robinson free to write.

It is fitting that Robinson wrote novels entitled *Housekeeping* and *Home*. She aligns herself with Emily Dickinson, approaching topics microscopically to unearth a "metonymy for the cosmos"—revealing the broadest meaning through detail. While she was at the Workshop, she wrote at home, moving around the house, from her study, to her couch, to wherever else might suit, so as not to feel bound by any particular location. But it was crucial to her to stay inside her house, so that she could forget her surroundings, and she dressed "like a bum," in order to be just as forgetful of her physical self.

If she wrote something she didn't like, she started anew without compunction, or scrapped the project altogether. She didn't generally feel the need to revise once the words were on the page, but would sit on her couch and worry over a paragraph until lunch, then return to the couch to worry about the same paragraph until supper. She might go days without hearing another human voice and not notice, and described herself as having "benevolent insomnia," waking in the night to write when the world was quiet, with a preternaturally clear mind.

Edith Wharton

Born: January 24, 1862, New York City
Died: August 11, 1937, Saint-Brice-sous-Forêt, France

The Mount, Lenox, Massachusetts

"[T]he Mount was my first real home," wrote Wharton. After publication of *The House of Mirth* (1905), she had publicity photos taken of her working at a desk in the Mount's library, but she actually worked on her books in her bedroom. She wrote in bed, mostly in the morning, in longhand on numbered pages, with a wooden desk balanced on her knees.

"Set wide the window. Let me drink the day."

—Edith Wharton

Great wealth can be a sort of prison. This was particularly true for women born in the nineteenth century. Edith Wharton (née Jones) came from a prominent New York City family, about whom the phrase "keeping up with the Joneses" is reputed to have originated, but though much was expected of her, becoming a literary figure did not count among these expectations. (Her mother even forbade her from reading novels until she had married.)

The era's exhausting, stultifying standards of societal etiquette and decorum rankled Wharton from the start, for she had ideas of her own. "[I]t must never be forgotten that every one is unconsciously tyrannized over by the wants of others," she wrote in *The Decoration of Houses* (1897), her first major success as a writer. In this book, cowritten with architect Ogden Codman, she railed against ponderous Victorian homes and advocated for spaces laid out with attention to symmetry and lightness, in the classical style.

In 1901, she put these philosophies into practice, when she and her husband bought 113 acres in Lenox, Massachusetts. Wharton set about designing, with Codman, a house and grounds that met her aesthetical, social, and creative needs, as she described in her 1934 memoir, *A Backward Glance*:

> On a slope overlooking the dark waters and densely wooded shores of Laurel Lake we built a spacious and dignified house, to which we gave the name of my great-grandfather's place, the Mount. . . . There for over ten years I lived and gardened and wrote contentedly.

A proliferation of doors led from the Mount's cavernous entrance hall, up the staircase to a gallery, through a drawing room, and into Wharton's library, where only a select few were allowed. For Wharton, this largely involved her literary circle, particularly Henry James, who was "first on the list of the friends who composed my closest group during the years I spent there, and those that followed."

Having felt hemmed in all of her life, she was finally free—to an extent. "I should have preferred to live [there] all the year round . . . but my husband's fondness for society, and his dislike of the New England winter cold, made this impossible." They therefore spent summers in the Mount and winters at their "small house" in New York, or off on their many trips to Europe. Wharton later wistfully recalled "long days at the Mount, in the deep summer glow or the crisp glitter of autumn, the walks in the woods, motor-flights over hill and dale, evening talks on the moonlit terrace and readings around the library fire."

Wharton penned two seminal novels at the Mount, *The House of Mirth* and *Ethan Frome*. Were it not for her husband's failing mental health and their subsequent faltering marriage, she likely would have lived there for the remainder of her life. But, as she wrote in her memoir, twenty years after moving out, "its blessed influence still lives in me."

"Perhaps home is not a place but simply an irrevocable condition."

—James Baldwin

"The ache for home lives in all of us. The safe place where we can go as we are and not be questioned."

—Maya Angelou

"I think you travel to search and you come back home to find yourself there."

—Chimamanda Ngozi Adichie

Alice Munro

Born: July 10, 1931, Wingham, Ontario

1648 Rockland Avenue, Victoria, British Columbia

Munro described a story as being like a house you enter, roam around in, settle in for a while. The author has to gather material to build that house, to make it into somewhere someone would wish to be. The Munros threw parties in their house. Sometimes writers would stop by. Margaret Atwood visited once. She sat cross-legged on the floor and did Sheila's horoscope.

> "People are curious. A few people are. They will be
> driven to find things out, even trivial things."
>
> —Alice Munro

In 1966, Alice Munro's thirteen-year-old daughter, Sheila, spotted an ad for a mansion: a twelve-room Tudor Revival built in 1894. It was the type of house that had fallen out of fashion at the time (everyone wanted to move to the suburbs), and having been turned into a duplex, it was in a state of disrepair. It had potential, but would need a lot of work to restore it to its former glory. There were five fireplaces, twelve-foot ceilings, and a nanny's quarters that could be turned into bedrooms for the children. The gardens had once been beautiful. Munro's husband and children loved the house, but Munro herself, then eight months pregnant, was not convinced. She eventually agreed, reluctantly, but made Sheila promise she would do all the vacuuming.

The Munros had moved to Victoria, British Columbia, in 1963, and opened a bookstore they called Munro's Books. In an upstairs room of the house, Munro installed a typewriter on a table. She would usually try to write in the morning, before going to work at the shop in the afternoons. But for the year after her baby was born, she was exhausted. Coming home after a day at the store, she would immediately have to get supper ready. She grew discouraged, and the house seemed to amplify the problems in her marriage. She felt the need to move on.

In 1967, a publisher asked Munro to put together a collection of stories for a book. She spent that winter collecting pieces written over the past fourteen years, and writing three new ones. The book, *Dance of the Happy Shades*, published the following year, didn't sell well, but it won the Governor General's Award, which finally forced Munro to admit to people that she spent her mornings writing stories, rather than making curtains, as she had previously claimed. For the 1971 census, she listed herself as a "writer" rather than a "housewife."

Munro (a consummate reviser) spent that year typing out draft after draft of her next book, *Lives of Girls and Women*, writing during the cold months on a table in the laundry room, where heat from the dryer compensated for the failings of the house's antiquated furnace. She found herself unable to write if there was another adult in the house, as though still embarrassed to be writing at all. And she needed a long period of aimless thought, staring at the wall, in order to work out the details of a story. The first draft came slowly, about seven hundred words a day, and by the final draft she was working twelve to fourteen hours a day. She had worked on the book nearly every day for a year. Her writing life was now established—but her marriage was coming to an end.

The Munros separated in 1972. For a while, Munro lived in an apartment and came home to cook for the family. The final break came in 1973, when she was offered a job teaching creative writing in Nelson, British Columbia, and left with her children to make a new life.

Chimamanda Ngozi Adichie

Born: September 15, 1977, Enugu, Enugu State, Nigeria

305 Marguerite Cartwright Avenue, University of Nigeria, Nsukka, Nigeria

After independence from the United Kingdom in 1960, the Nigerian government set up its first indigenous university in Nsukka. Adichie's father was one of its first professors, and as he rose through the academic ranks, they were moved to progressively bigger houses on campus, 305 being the last and grandest. Adichie has written that there must have been literary spirits in the bathroom, as she often got ideas for stories while taking baths there.

> **"I saw that my life was a vast glowing empty page and I could do anything I wanted."**
>
> —Jack Kerouac

In January 1951, Beat writer John Clellon Holmes told Neal Cassady, who was passing through town (always passing through), that their friend Jack Kerouac was struggling in his quest to write the book he had already titled *On the Road* (1957)—the true story of their trips across America and Mexico. To which Cassady responded, "Gee, man, that's fine, but you don't make no dough that way!"

Kerouac had just moved with his new wife, Joan Haverty, to New York City at 454 West 20th Street, the second floor of a tree-shaded four-story brownstone across from a Protestant seminary in Chelsea (which at the time was a working-class neighborhood). Haverty had rented the apartment after becoming fed up with sharing a home with Kerouac's mother.

Though Kerouac may not have been making any dough with his writing at the time, he was at least earning fifty dollars a week writing script synopses for 20th Century Fox. And this went a long way in Chelsea. Allen Ginsberg, for example, was paying $4.50 a week for an attic room a ten-minute walk away, on 15th Street.

The time was right. He had been planning this novel a long time, drawing up notes, sketching out chapters. But first he had an innovation. Before starting, he cut sheets of tracing paper into long strips, just the right width for his typewriter, and taped them together into a 120-foot-long roll, which he then fed into the machine. This allowed him to type continuously. And thus began a three-week flurry of writing/typing (Ginsberg claimed Kerouac to be a 128-word-a-minute typist), and the creation of what is likely the most totem-like item in all of modern literature—manuscript as scroll, with no chapter or paragraph breaks, and scarce few commas.

When Holmes visited Kerouac's apartment on the morning of April 9, 1951, he had to wake Jack, who had gone to sleep only a few hours before. Kerouac had been up all night writing, and said he had already clocked in thirty-four thousand words, Joan at hand (not entirely happily) to feed him endless cups of coffee and bowls of pea soup. But this didn't mean he was so busy that he couldn't join his friends out on the town. He and other Beats walked along the river, or sat on Chelsea's deserted wharves and talked about literature and life. And they drank. A lot.

But despite these breaks, Kerouac did inflict a punishing schedule on himself over these weeks, in order to get what he had been after for so long: a paean to his generation, and to that indelibly American urge, to move and not settle, to owe no one anything, and—no matter the cost—to be free.

An edited version was published six years later. Names were changed, probably necessary for legal reasons, much of the sex was scrubbed (to avoid the censor's knife, but also so as not to offend his mother), and the word "holy" was sprinkled throughout the text as a way of delineating the quasi-spiritual nature of his intentions.

Margaret Atwood

Born: November 18, 1939, Ottawa, Canada

Helmstedter Strasse 27, West Berlin, West Germany

Atwood wrote the first draft of *The Handmaid's Tale* by hand on yellow legal notepads. She then typed up this draft using a large German-keyboard manual typewriter she had rented. She then wrote notes on the typed pages, and finally she gave this second draft to a professional typist. Atwood left Berlin in June 1984, returning to Canada (and, eventually, Alabama) to finish the book.

"War is what happens when language fails."

—Margaret Atwood

By the mid-1980s, there was a significant amount of pushback against the gains that had been made by the women's movement during the 1970s. Margaret Atwood, witnessing this pushback, found a question persisting in her mind: how exactly would they go about reversing these gains? To provide a possible answer, she decided to write a novel.

Propitiously, this was around the time that she was invited by the German Academic Exchange Service (DAAD) to live and work in West Berlin for a few months, on a grant that provided funding for artists of all kinds to come to West Germany. The Federal Republic of Germany saw this as one way to help keep the citizens of the city—185 square miles walled off inside East Germany—connected to the world outside the Eastern Bloc.

It was the spring of 1984, and there was no end to the Cold War in sight. Although Atwood later referred to West Berlin as a showpiece for Western capitalist merchandising, she remembers it as being precarious, dark, and empty, with many vacant apartments, and populated by elderly women who had lived through the war and young men avoiding conscription into the Germany army. Every Sunday, her DAAD-owned apartment in the Bayerisches Viertel ("Bavarian Quarter") area of Schöneberg was rattled by sonic booms caused by East German jets flying exercises, carried out, no doubt, to remind the citizens of West Berlin of their presence—and their proximity.

But life continued as normally as it could. When not working, Atwood would walk around town to practice the German she had learned at school and university, and in this way, the particular tensions of West Berlin—and the parallel anxieties she encountered during the trips she took through East Germany, Czechoslovakia, and Poland—informed the world she was creating for her book. She bore witness to the fear of surveillance: the pointed silences in conversations, the changes of subject, the oblique manner in which people conveyed information.

All of this fed into the novel, which was initially called Offred, after the central character (and didn't receive its final name—*The Handmaid's Tale*—until January 1985, after almost 150 pages had been written). Atwood had been drawn to dystopian literature since childhood, having been particularly influenced by Aldous Huxley's *Brave New World* (1932), Ray Bradbury's *Fahrenheit 451* (1953), and—fittingly, given the year she began writing the book—George Orwell's *1984*. She was also fascinated by dictatorships, which she has noted may not be surprising for someone born three months after the outbreak of World War II, and who grew up aware that entrenched systems could disappear in the blink of an eye. She had never written speculative fiction, though, and she was concerned she might not be able for it. She decided she would make a rule for the novel: it would contain only the kinds of misdeeds that human beings had already perpetrated at some point in history, as a way of demonstrating just how easily we could make the same—or worse—mistakes all over again.

"With friends,
one is well;
but at home,
one is better."

—Leo Tolstoy

"For he came to perceive that since people were his study, his teachers, the objects through which he could satisfy his persistent wonder about life itself, his own being among others, wherever he lived for the moment, there was his home."

—Pearl S. Buck

Marcel Proust

Born: July 10, 1871, Auteuil, France
Died: November 18, 1922, Paris, France

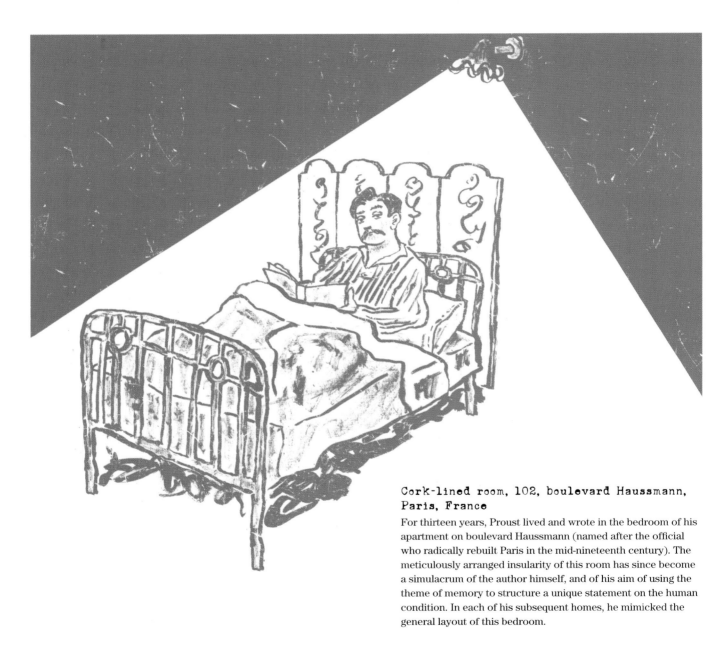

Cork-lined room, 102, boulevard Haussmann, Paris, France

For thirteen years, Proust lived and wrote in the bedroom of his apartment on boulevard Haussmann (named after the official who radically rebuilt Paris in the mid-nineteenth century). The meticulously arranged insularity of this room has since become a simulacrum of the author himself, and of his aim of using the theme of memory to structure a unique statement on the human condition. In each of his subsequent homes, he mimicked the general layout of this bedroom.

▲ Poet and playwright Friedrich von Schiller, whose collaboration with Goethe led to a renaissance of drama in Germany.

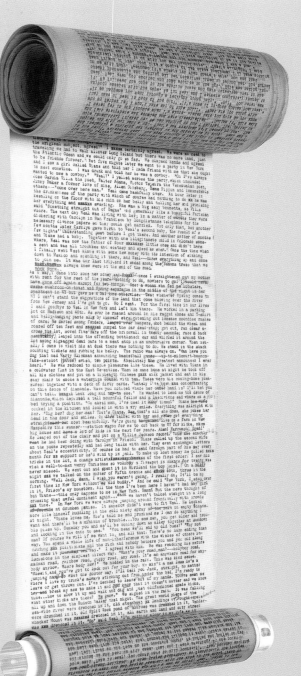

▲ As displayed on tour, a 36-foot section of the original 119 feet, 8 inches of nonstop, unedited writing that was the original *On the Road* manuscript.

desk." This allowed her to get close to her work, and to compose at different times of day. She copied her finished manuscripts from these scraps "in clear, legible, delicate traced writing, almost as easy to read as print."

Stimulants have often fueled the creative process. Throughout the course of the day, Truman Capote would progress from mint tea to sherry, and finally martinis, all of which consumed while lying down. Kingsley Amis found moderate amounts of alcohol, in the form of a glass of Scotch, to be "a sort of artistic ice-breaker." Aldous Huxley turned an afternoon's experiment with mescaline into his book *The Doors of Perception*. Perhaps strangest of all was the German poet Friedrich Schiller's habit of keeping a drawer full of rotten apples in his desk, the chemical effects of which induced a light-headed feeling he found to be essential to creation.

Judith Kerr

Born: June 14, 1923, Berlin, Germany
Died: May 22, 2019, London, UK

Top-floor studio, Barnes, London, UK

The millions of children and former children who have read Kerr's books would have instantly recognized the interior of her home from her drawings—the kitchen cabinets the tiger lay across while drinking the faucet dry, for example. Mog the cat, who lived to be almost twenty, visited the studio often, sitting on Kerr's lap and nudging the brush with its nose.

> "I walk about and look at people, out with their children, and I think, do they realise how fragile it all is?"
>
> —Judith Kerr

Judith Kerr followed up a tumultuous and terrifying start to her life with more than five decades of stability and contentedness. Her parents were Jewish and her father, a drama critic, had openly mocked the Nazis before they came to power. By 1933, it was clear that their family would have to flee Berlin. (The Nazis, who later burned Kerr's father's books, came for their passports the day after they crossed the border into Switzerland.) It wasn't until 1962 that Kerr put down roots, in Barnes, a quiet neighborhood in southwest London. Kerr found the area to be pretty rundown when she moved there with her husband, but they loved it nonetheless. They got a cat to help make their house a home, and named it Mog—short for "moggie," the feline equivalent of "mutt."

Under the eaves at the top of the house, up two flights of stairs (so that potential visitors would think twice before paying a visit), were two studies—or workrooms, as she called them—side by side, sharing a view over Barnes Common. The study used by Kerr's husband, Nigel Kneale, a writer of sci-fi and horror, had a typewriter and props from one of his television programs, including an alien that was missing a few legs. Kerr's workroom was completely white—walls, floorboards, furniture—and populated by hundreds of crayons, separated according to color in jars to keep track of them all.

Her drawing board was part of a desk she bought with the five pounds her brother gave her when she turned twenty. She later coated it with Formica, but otherwise it remained unchanged over the decades. Her walls were sparsely decorated: a poster for a reading from Kerr's father's books by a famous German actor, who would later do readings from Kerr's books as well; a straw hat her son brought back from some far-flung place. Soft sunlight filtered through the trees, and there were plenty of lamps to enable nighttime writing. If Kerr was particularly inspired she would work as late as five in the morning, but usually she would start at eleven in the morning and keep going until she ran out of ideas. Her wastepaper basket was in a constant state of overflow.

Either writer could pop into the other's room if they were stuck. Kneale would tell Kerr about a play he was writing, and she would show him her drawings; he might say something like, "Isn't that child's head too big?" As Kerr had found the English language difficult to learn, she used as few words as possible in her books, repeating them for comedic effect.

In more than five decades working here she produced some of the best-selling children's books of all time, including *The Tiger Who Came to Tea* (1968) (instigated by her son refusing to read another word of the boring children's books on offer), *Mog the Forgetful Cat* (1970) (the first of seventeen Mog books), and *When Hitler Stole Pink Rabbit* (1971) (inspired by her family's experience fleeing Nazi-era Germany).

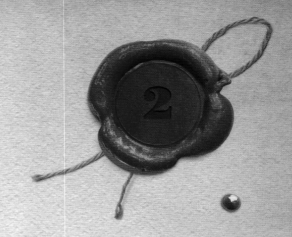

Sanctuary in the City

(Samuel) Dashiell Hammett

Born: May 27, 1894, St. Mary's County, Virginia
Died: January 8, 1961, New York City

Tall, thin, witty, distinguished, Hammett the man brought almost as much character to the New York and Hollywood scene of the interwar years as his great creations Sam Spade and Ned Beaumont brought to detective fiction. An ex-private detective himself and master of a spare, direct prose style, Hammett scored a huge success with his third novel, *The Maltese Falcon*, published in 1930 and reprinted seven times that year.

This success led to him laying aside work on *The Thin Man* (a novel he would eventually publish in 1934) and decamping to Hollywood to write movie scripts for David O. Selznick of Paramount. This move resulted in his movie *City Streets*, starring Gary Cooper. The following year, his novel *The Glass Key* was published to even greater accolades than those that had greeted *The Maltese Falcon*—"about twice as good" was the opinion of the critic at the *New York Herald Tribune*.

**The Sutton Club Hotel,
330 East 56th Street, New York City**

The hotel, located on a broad residential street leading down to the East River, began life in 1929 but was already a somewhat shabby affair when it opened its doors to Dash Hammett and Lillian Hellman three years later. He had left his previous hotel, the Pierre, without paying his bill and was wearing all his clothes, so a room at the Sutton, for all its tight space and mean furniture, must have seemed a welcome refuge. More importantly, the ambience was congenial: the manager was Nathanael West, self-styled as "P.N. West, the great writer and bordello keeper"—some of the guests were prostitutes, others his writer friends. Here, in one of the cramped rooms jokingly known as the "diplomat suite," Hammett turned his earlier idea for *The Thin Man* into a fully fledged novel.

"... he is a good, hell-bent, cold-hearted writer, with a clear eye for the ways of hard women and a fine ear for the words of hard men, and his books are exciting and powerful ... "

—Dorothy Parker

Hammett easily took to the Hollywood lifestyle, living grandly in hotel suites, wearing beautiful clothes, splashing out on lavish presents, and partying hard with fellow script-writers, starlets, and other glitterati. He also found a new lover in the shape of the feisty and funny Lillian Hellman, an aspiring playwright who was to prove herself the best friend of a lifetime.

But extravagance and heavy drinking took their toll. In poor shape (he also suffered from tuberculosis) and badly in need of funds, Hammett returned to the calmer waters of New York in 1932. Here he had to leave one hotel after another as he was unable to pay the bills. Now there was only one place he could go: the Sutton Club Hotel on East 56th Street in Midtown Manhattan.

This rundown hotel had an unusual manager in Nathanael West, himself a novelist and scriptwriter, who let out the small, uncomfortable rooms at a cheap rent to friends and fellow authors. Hammett and Hellmann took one each. Sustained by a small publisher's advance, Hammett shut himself away to rewrite and complete *The Thin Man*. Hellmann was astonished at the change in his working practice: "The drinking stopped, the parties were over. The locking-in time had come and nothing was allowed to disturb it until the book was finished." She much admired the care he lavished not only on the writing itself but on each meticulously typewritten page.

The Thin Man introduces Nick Charles, an alcoholic ex-detective married to the younger, sophisticated Nora. They are a couple who really get along, and their charac-ters and repartee owe something to Lillian and Hammett's own. Nick, on Christmas vacation in New York with Nora, is sought out to solve the mystery of an inventor's dis-appearance after his secretary has been murdered. He reluctantly agrees, painstakingly seeking out the truth against a backdrop of hectic partying. The treatment is light and amusing, but the view of human behavior remains bleak: avarice and self-interest rule as much in the world of the socialite as in the hoodlum's.

The book, published in 1934, was an instant bestseller, and MGM paid Hammett $21,000 for the film rights. Shot in eighteen days, the movie, in its turn, was such a success that five more Thin Man movies followed. Hammett wrote three of the screenplays—but no more novels, following his own wise advice that, "If you are tired you ought to rest, I think, and not try to fool yourself and your customers with colored bubbles."

Ray Bradbury

Born: August 22, 1920, Waukegan, Illinois
Died: June 5, 2012, Los Angeles, California

Powell Library, University of California, Los Angeles

Constructed in the late 1920s, this library, built in the Romanesque Revival style, was one of the UCLA campus's original four buildings. Bradbury, as he put it later, literally wrote a dime novel in its basement, overseen by tens of thousands of books. He estimated that he spent $9.80 writing the first draft of *Fahrenheit 451*, dime by dime by dime.

"In science fiction, we dream."

—Ray Bradbury

In the 1940s, Ray Bradbury had already found some success as a writer. A young editorial assistant named Truman Capote had saved Bradbury's story "Homecoming" from *Mademoiselle* magazine's "slush pile," and it went on to win an O. Henry Award in 1947. But Bradbury was still scrabbling to make a living. His next idea was to expand upon one of his previously published stories, "Bright Phoenix," particularly its theme of book burning. He thought he had enough for a novella set in a futuristic dystopia where books and learning are forbidden. And he had a title for it: *The Fireman*. Now he just needed a place to write it.

From as early as 1941, Bradbury had done most of his writing in his garage. In early 1950, he and his family were living in a tract house in Venice, a seaside neighborhood in southwest Los Angeles, and Bradbury's two young children were prone to tapping on the garage windows, singing to their father and asking him to play with them. He decided the temptation to shirk his writing (their only income at the time) was too great, but he didn't have enough money to rent an office; he was going to have to find a cheap alternative.

Unusually for an Angeleno, Bradbury didn't have a driver's license, and instead he often cycled wherever he needed to go. One day he ended up on the campus of UCLA, where he wandered into the Powell Library. Bradbury himself had eschewed college to pursue his dream of becoming a writer. He wasn't against learning, but he had grown up during the Great Depression, and his family didn't have a lot of money, so it was less of a viable option. And besides, he preferred to do his learning on his own—in libraries.

Powell Library was modeled after the Basilica of Sant'Ambrogio in Milan, Italy, which makes it essentially a cathedral of books—a fitting location for someone so enamored with the power and importance of the written word. As Bradbury roamed the corridors, gazing at the titles on the stacks, he heard the sound of typing rising through the floor. In the library's basement, he found neat rows of tables holding old Remington and Underwood typewriters, which could be rented for ten cents a half hour, and eight or nine students working furiously. Bradbury rushed off to the bank to get a bag of dimes, then got to work.

He described himself as driven crazy when his typewriter jammed, whipping pages in and out of the device. Between dime drops he would wander upstairs to find quotes for his book and, thus inspired, run back to the basement for another half-hour burst of typing. Within nine days, he had finished a twenty-five-thousand-word first draft. *The Fireman* was published in *Galaxy Science Fiction* magazine in 1951. Urged by his publishers to double the length of his story to make a novel, Bradbury went back to the typing room and turned his novella into *Fahrenheit 451* (1953), again taking just nine days.

Honoré de Balzac

Born: May 20, 1799, Tours, France
Died: August 18, 1850, Paris, France

47, rue Raynouard, Passy, Paris

From 1840 to 1847, this apartment served Honoré de Balzac as a refuge from the city, where he could pace the floor for hours on end in the middle of the night, drinking cup after cup of coffee, searching for the perfect phrase. This sole survivor of Balzac's three Parisian residences now serves as a museum to the author.

> "Solitude is fine, but you need someone to
> tell you that solitude is fine."

—Honoré de Balzac

In November 1840, Honoré de Balzac wrote to Eveline Hańska, the Polish noblewoman he would marry ten years later, instructing her to "write me at the following address: M. de Breugnol, rue Basse, n19 in Passy, near Paris. I am there, hidden for some time. . . . It was necessary for me to move very quickly and I am locked in where I am."

The apartment at 19, rue Basse, which has since become 47, rue Raynouard, was in the town of Passy, near the Bois de Boulogne, which at the time was outside the city of Paris proper. Balzac's reasons for subterfuge were financial, and he rented the property under his housekeeper's name in an attempt to elude his many creditors.

In the decades and centuries before Balzac moved there, Passy had transformed from a bucolic hilltop village above the river Seine, populated by farmers and quarrymen, into terraces of modest houses and elegant hotels. During the mid-nineteenth century, many of these buildings began to be rented to members of the rising classes—such as Balzac, whose apartment was an annex of one of these hotels. To gain access, Balzac had to enter through a separate building and descend a few flights of stone steps, which arrived at a courtyard garden opposite what appeared to be a one-story cottage, but which was built onto the edge of a steep slope, extending downward.

One of the apartment's five rooms was a study, featuring stained-glass windows, Versailles parquet flooring, and a black marble fireplace. Its walls were hung with red velvet tied with black silk cords, and a portrait of Madame Hańksa. Most importantly, this is where visitors would find Balzac's armchair and his work table, of which he wrote: "I possessed it for ten years, it saw all of my misery, wiped away all of my tears, knew all of my projects, heard all of my thoughts. My arm almost wore it out moving back and forth over it as I wrote." With him there would also have been his signature turquoise-studded walking cane, as well as a very well-used coffee pot.

In this study he labored over his works for the next seven years, editing *La Comédie humaine*, his enormous, and never completed, series of intellectual novels and stories that Balzac intended to cover the gamut of human existence—his masterpiece—and writing some of the most celebrated novels in the series, including *Une ténébreuse affaire, La Rabouilleuse*, and *La Cousine Bette*. Balzac worked ceaselessly, and his work habits are legendary. It was not unusual for him to write for seven hours straight—beginning at one o'clock in the morning. He tended to write in bursts of activity, and at great speed, with a quill. He claimed to have once written for forty-eight hours, interrupted only by three hours of sleep.

In part due to this chaotic writing schedule, Balzac never spent as much time in the salons of Paris as did his characters. As the author George Saintsbury wrote in his introduction to a late-nineteenth-century edition of *La Comédie humaine*, Balzac "felt it was his business not to frequent society but to create it."

". . . to each man a city consists of no more than a few streets, a few houses, a few people. Remove those few and a city exists no longer except as a pain in the memory . . ."

—Graham Greene

"A city has to be a place where you can get everything—and do anything, or nothing."

—Herbert Eugene Caen

"Don't let the wicked city get you down."

—Sylvia Plath

"Cities are the abyss of the human species."

—Jean-Jacques Rousseau

Arthur C. Clarke

Born: December 16, 1917, Minehead, UK
Died: March 19, 2008, Colombo, Sri Lanka

Chelsea Hotel, 222 West 23rd Street, New York City

In 1965, the same year that Bob Dylan wrote "Visions of Johanna" at the hotel, Clarke labored here over *2001: A Space Odyssey*, living on crackers, tea, and pâté. Distractions abounded at the Chelsea, but the ever-fastidious Clarke was able to block them out—though he would occasionally entertain himself by shooting a laser beam onto the sidewalk far below, just to bewilder pedestrians.

> "Perhaps our role on this planet is not to worship God-but to create Him."
>
> —Arthur C. Clarke

In terms of creativity per square foot, no location can compete with the Chelsea Hotel. Built in 1884 as one of New York City's first apartment cooperatives, it operated under a progressive spirit from the start. Murals covered the walls of the common dining room, where, in 1888, Mark Twain read aloud from *A Connecticut Yankee in King Arthur's Court*, to an audience that included fellow author William Dean Howells. After the cooperative went bankrupt in 1905, the building was converted into a luxury hotel; by the middle of the twentieth century, the luxury had faded, whereas the Chelsea's reputation as a refuge for writers, artists, and musicians was stronger than ever. Dylan Thomas stayed at the Chelsea in 1953, during his final, fatal trip to America, and in the early 1960s, the Irish writer Brendan Behan could often be heard loudly reciting poetry in the corridors, to cite just two examples.

By 1965, Arthur C. Clarke was a Chelsea regular. In 1958, while staying at the Chelsea, Clarke had been called in to lead a panel in support of William Burroughs, another frequent Chelsea guest, after censorship of a magazine publishing excerpts of Burroughs's novel *Naked Lunch*. Clarke called the Chelsea his "spiritual home." He had made the hotel his American base during his increasingly frequent tours lecturing on the Space Age, about which he had quickly become an expert, having been perhaps the first person to predict the creation of a network of communications satellites.

In 1964, Clarke met with filmmaker Stanley Kubrick in New York to discuss collaborating on a sci-fi film. Although they were opposites in temperament—Kubrick, a bombastic night owl New Yorker, and Clarke, a reserved, polite Englishman who tended not to stay up past ten—they got on well from the start. Initially they planned on having Clarke write the screenplay, but Kubrick suggested that they instead write a novel, on which they would base the film. They brainstormed in Clarke's tidy top-floor Chelsea Hotel apartment, reviewing all of Clarke's short stories to see which they could expand and convert into a film. They eventually settled on "The Sentinel," about an alien object discovered on the moon; their working title for the film was *How the Solar System Was Won*.

Writing at the blistering pace of two thousand words a day on his gray Smith Corona typewriter, Clarke was at pains to create a plot for the film that would please the notoriously punctilious director. A friend and fellow Chelsea resident, the author Terry Southern, had worked with Kubrick on his film *Dr. Strangelove* (1964), three years previous, and he sympathized with Clarke. To relieve the stress, Clarke would take breaks with another Chelsea resident, the playwright Arthur Miller, at the Horn & Hardart Automat on Seventh Avenue, where patrons dropped nickels into slots in exchange for breakfast, and Clarke would fill Miller's ears with predictions of vast space colonies.

"In town a man can live for a hundred years without noticing that he has long been dead and has rotten away."

—Leo Tolstoy

"In New York the opportunities for learning, and acquiring a culture that shall not come out of the ruins, but belong to life, are probably greater than anywhere else in the world."

—Thomas Wolfe

"It was in those days when I wandered about hungry in Kristiania, that strange city which no one leaves before it has set its mark upon him. . ."

—Knut Hamsun

Franz Kafka

Born: July 3, 1883, Prague, Bohemia (now Czech Republic)
Died: June 3, 1924, Kierling, Austria

No. 22 Zlatá ulička (Golden Lane) Prague, Czech Republic

The low ceilings, small windows, and plain fortified walls of this medieval house would have provided Franz Kafka with a welcome refuge from the distractions and clamor of his home in the Old Town, in the center of Prague. It gave him plenty of time, in the small hours of night, when he chose to write, to contemplate the horrors of existence.

> "How about if I sleep a little bit longer
> and forget all this nonsense . . ."
>
> —Franz Kafka

In 1913, Franz Kafka was promoted to junior secretary at the Worker's Accident Insurance Institute. His new shift began at eight in the morning and ended at two or two-thirty in the afternoon, giving him, theoretically, ample time to write. But first there was lunch, after which he would attempt to sleep, disturbed by his frequent headaches or a panoply of other maladies, until about seven-thirty in the evening. Afterward he would go for a walk, often with his friend Max Brod (who, after Kafka's death—thankfully, for us—would defy the author's wish to have his remaining manuscripts burned), followed by dinner with his sisters and parents. Only then, at ten-thirty or eleven, would he finally sit down to write, until two or three in the morning (and sometimes as late as six), if he found the strength.

These difficulties, along with the brevity of the author's life and his penchant for putting flames to pieces he found disagreeable (which is to say, nearly all of them), help to explain why so few of his works survive. As Kafka wrote to Felice Bauer, to whom he was twice engaged but never married, "time is short, my strength is limited, the office is a horror, the apartment is noisy, and if a pleasant, straightforward life is not possible then one must try to wriggle through by subtle maneuvers."

Having lived the majority of his life in the Old Town, in the noisy center of Prague, most often in cramped circumstances with his family, Kafka found that this straightforward life lay mostly outside of his reach. But he was to have a short reprieve from the distractions of the city in 1916, when the youngest of his three sisters, Ottla, with whom he had the closest relationship, rented a small house at no. 22 Zlatá ulička (Golden Lane), within the northern wall of Prague Castle.

Taking its name from the goldsmiths who once lived there, Golden Lane reaches a dead end at Daliborka Tower, formerly a dungeon. The humble houses that line the street, dating from the 1600s, were originally built for the castle's archers, though their services were no longer required by the time they were installed there, and the street soon fell into poverty, becoming a place of residence for laborers and artists.

Kafka wrote at no. 22 until early 1917, when he was diagnosed with tuberculosis and moved to the countryside to convalesce. The disease would take his life seven years later. It is apt, then, that "A Country Doctor," written here as part of a story collection of the same name in the midst of World War I, tells a tale of the failure of modern medicine. Uncharacteristically, Kafka was vaguely pleased with his work. As he wrote in 1917, "I can still have temporary satisfaction from works like 'A Country Doctor,' assuming I achieve anything more of the sort (very unlikely); but happiness only if I can raise the world into the pure, the true, the unchangeable."

Toni Morrison

Born: February 18, 1931, Lorain, Ohio
Died: August 5, 2019, New York City

Couch, sunrise, Syracuse, New York

During her eighteen months in Syracuse, Morrison edited textbooks, seeking to revise the way African Americans were presented in the curriculum, and job and family responsibilities forced her to write in the small hours. After *The Bluest Eye* was published in 1970, she told no one at her work, though they found out soon enough—after a review appeared in the *New York Times*.

> "The vitality of language lies in its ability to limn the actual, imagined and possible lives of its speakers, readers, writers."
>
> —Toni Morrison

In the summer of 1964, Toni Morrison traveled to Europe with her husband and infant son. By the time she returned, she was divorced. With no job prospects, a child to look after, and another on the way, she went to her parents' home in Lorain to consider her options. The following winter, she spotted an ad in the *New York Review of Books* for a job as an editor at a textbook company, a subsidiary of Random House in Syracuse, New York.

Morrison took the job in part because Random House assured her she would eventually be transferred to their headquarters in New York City. As a result, she made no effort to find new friends in Syracuse, and after Morrison's children went to sleep at seven in the evening, there followed long nights of loneliness and unhappiness. She needed a book to keep her company. A book about people who were African American and young and lived in the Midwest. But authors rarely wrote about these people, and whenever they did, the characters were little more than background scenery. She decided she would write the book herself—using her solitude to invent company.

That first snowy winter, she picked up again a story about a black girl who wished she had blue eyes, which she'd begun in a writer's group in 1962, while teaching at Howard University. Morrison thought she could turn it into a novel. At first, she wrote in the evenings, once the children were asleep. But given her multiple responsibilities, she knew her writing time would be sporadic, so she grabbed time whenever she could. She soon found that she wrote best before dawn, waking at four in the morning to work in the living room, often recumbent on her couch, getting as much done as possible before her children called out for her (as early as five o'clock).

Writers devise ways to transform themselves into a conduit for words. For Morrison, light was the catalyst—being there before it arrived; being there as it happened. She found that watching the sun rise with a cup of coffee triggered the flow of words. And if discouragement reared its ugly head, she considered her grandmother, who had fled the South with seven children and no means of support. Any existential fretting—about money, about her parenting, about writing—dissipated in the knowledge that every problem was surmountable.

She also took strength from her work in publishing. It decreased her awe of the industry. She understood the adversarial relationship that can arise between writers and publishers. She knew, being one herself, how critical an editor was (and she would later have one of the best of the era, in Robert Gottlieb). In 1968, Morrison left Syracuse for New York City, where Random House quickly gave her a position working with mass-market fiction and nonfiction, developing books that helped shape the literary world and editing titles by cultural titans such as Muhammad Ali and Angela Davis, before giving up editing in order to become a cultural titan in her own right.

Sylvia Plath

Born: October 27, 1932, Boston, Massachusetts
Died: February 11, 1963, London

**The Barbizon Hotel for Women,
140 East 63rd Street, New York City**

Plath stayed here in a small room on the fifteenth floor for a
month in the summer after her third year at Smith College,
hoping that her guest editorship of *Mademoiselle* magazine
might catapult her into a literary life. She wrote at her desk at
night, looking into New York's network of lights, the sound of
car horns drifting up "like the sweetest music."

> *"Perhaps when we find ourselves wanting everything, it is because we are dangerously near to wanting nothing."*
>
> —Sylvia Plath

On May 31, 1953, Sylvia Plath strode out of New York City's Grand Central Terminal flanked by two soldiers she'd met on the train from Massachusetts. Burdened with Plath's luggage, the soldiers accompanied her all the way to the Barbizon Hotel for Women, where she was staying. It was her first time in the city; *Mademoiselle*, a New York-based magazine geared towards young women, at the time held an annual national competition for high-school graduates to serve as a guest editor for a month, and Plath, as that year's winning entry, was given a room at the Barbizon at the reduced rate of fifteen dollars a week.

The Barbizon, built in 1926 as a "Club Residence for Professional Women," was a twenty-three-story brick-and-sandstone tower faced in salmon-colored brick, with limestone and terra-cotta decorative elements in the neo-Gothic style. Standing on the corner of Lexington Avenue and 63rd Street on Manhattan's Upper East Side, the hotel had a swimming pool, a library, a bar, a formal dining room, a solarium, and athletic courts.

Part of the Barbizon's draw was its exclusivity, and its reputation for allowing only the most stylish of young women through its doors. But for all its desirability, it was also extremely restrictive. In order to secure one of its seven hundred tiny, dormitory-style rooms, a woman needed three letters of recommendation, and, once admitted, had to follow strict guidelines of decorum and dress (girdles, kitten heels, crisp skirts or suits). Parents paying for their daughter's stay could require that she sign in and out at the front desk, and they could even ask for her to be assigned a chaperone. Residents found in breach of the rules were reprimanded.

Recitals, theater readings, afternoon tea, bridge games, and other activities were held in the hotel's lounges, where the girls were allowed to host suitors (if they acquired a pass). Men weren't allowed beyond the grand lobby, with its stately staircase, rich furnishings, and Oriental carpets, but they often lurked in the ground-floor café, hoping to mingle with the hotel's elegant denizens. J. D. Salinger, who had lived a ten-minute walk from the Barbizon before leaving the city forever in January of that year, was once a regular there. Plath had asked *Mademoiselle* to set up an interview with Salinger for her, but, perhaps due to his absenting of the city, they paired her with the Irish novelist Elizabeth Bowen instead.

Plath's small room on the fifteenth floor had beige walls trimmed in maroon paint, a dark-green carpet, a bedspread with rose-patterned ruffles, and a green upholstered parlor chair. A speaker above the bed played classical music at the turn of a knob, and an enameled sink sprouted from one wall "like a convenient mushroom"—useful for washing out the white cotton gloves Barbizonians were expected to wear. Her room faced east, overlooking gardens and alleys, the Third Avenue El, the new United Nations building, and glimpses of the East River. Wedged neatly at the foot of Plath's bed was a desk for typing, where she wrote at night.

Plath left her room's windows permanently open that June, as New York was in the middle of a heat wave. The humidity added to the hotel's claustrophobic atmosphere, super-heating the ambition and anxiety prevalent among the eager young women compressed within. Although she found her month in New York invigorating (writing in a letter that her world had split open and "spilt out its guts like a watermelon"), years later, writing her only novel, *The Bell Jar* (1963, though not published in the US until 1971), she would play up the hotel's tropical aspects, and its concomitant stultifying, Darwinian connotations, by dubbing the hotel "The Amazon."

Plath, then just twenty, was reading James Joyce's *Ulysses* and wondering how she might go about writing a novel. She had won a string of academic prizes, had had several poems published, and was looking to convert this success into a tangible writing life. But for her month in New York she wanted to be social, keeping her door open at the Barbizon. She refused to take taxis, walking everywhere, even at five in the morning after a full night of drinking and dancing in Greenwich Village's jazz clubs. She ate at the Oyster Bar in Grand Central, drank cocktails at swanky rooftop bars, went to a Yankees game. At a lunch laid out by an advertising agency, she and several other Barbizonians got food poisoning from seafood, laying her low for a few days.

At *Mademoiselle*, she was asked to critique manuscripts by authors such as Noël Coward and Dylan Thomas. Plath greatly admired Thomas (with whom she shared a birthday), and, as luck would have it, he was in the city that month; he even visited *Mademoiselle*'s office, but, unfortunately, Plath wasn't there at the time. Determined to meet him, she and a few fellow Barbizonians lingered for six hours at the White Horse Tavern, his favorite bar in the city, but to no avail. They then went to the Chelsea Hotel, where he was staying, and camped out in the hallway next to his room overnight, but again he was a no-show.

On Plath's last night at the Barbizon, there was a party in someone's room, with lots of champagne, some wine, the odd bottle of liquor. Giddy and tipsy, Plath went to her room, grabbed her suitcase, and rode the elevator to the roof, where she sent each and every Barbizon-approved piece of clothing sailing off into the night. This event would later be immortalized in *The Bell Jar* as the moment that she freed herself from the constraints laid upon women in society. It was only as the champagne wore off that it occurred to Plath that she would need an outfit for the following day. She knocked on someone's door and asked to borrow an outfit, and was given a dirndl skirt and a "peasant-style" blouse. And so it was that, although Plath arrived in New York looking every part the New Yorker—modish, urbane, confident—she left the city tired, disheveled, and fragile.

MacDowell and Yaddo

A forest hideaway has nourished, for more than a century, eminent writers, or those about to become eminent. Created out of tragic family circumstances, in the idyllic surroundings of Saratoga Springs, New York, literary ideas have emerged that have won a multitude of awards.

I n 1896, Marian MacDowell, a pianist, and her husband Edward, a composer, bought a farm in Peterborough, New Hampshire, where they spent summers working. Not long after, Edward fell mortally ill, and told his wife that he wished to create a space where other artists could benefit from the farm's bucolic surroundings. Marian set about fulfilling his wish, garnering their vision national attention, and, in 1906, a fund was created in Edward's honor, bringing to life what would be called the MacDowell Colony. Thirty-two studios were built, scattered throughout the surrounding forest, and an artistic program was developed and flourished. On most years, three hundred or so artists, musicians, and writers came to work in peace. Thornton Wilder, who attended MacDowell nine times over three decades, based his play *Our Town* on Peterborough, writing much of it while in residence in June 1937. Marian ran MacDowell until her death in 1957, maintaining a firm set of rules, particularly in regard to female fellows: no wearing pants, smoking in public, or other transgressions, or you were out. In subsequent decades the spirit created by the MacDowells was retained, while the rules fell away. In 2020, MacDowell dropped "Colony" from its name for its unsavory historical connotations.

▲ The pergola at Yaddo. The Trasks designed Yaddo's garden themselves, and Katrina's aim for it "was not to be distinctly Italian nor French nor English. It was to be Yaddo." The pergola divides the more formal lower terrace of the garden, with its rose garden and fountain, from the woodland rock garden.

Yaddo was the Saratoga Springs, New York, estate of financier Spencer Trask and his wife Katrina, a writer. The name "Yaddo" was created by their daughter, a neologism meant to rhyme with "shadow." Left without heirs after the deaths of their four children, the Trasks bequeathed their estate to the establishment of a

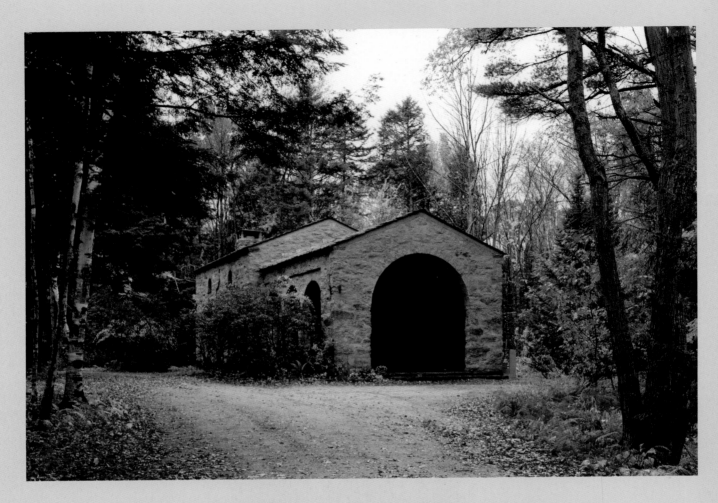

▲ The Alexander Studio at MacDowell, completed in 1922, was originally designed to be an art gallery. Renovated in 1993, it is now one of thirty-two studios at MacDowell for use by established and emerging artists in a range of disciplines, including music composition, architecture, literature, and the visual arts.

residency program for artists. Yaddo opened its doors to its first group of guests in 1926, by which time both Trasks had died. Yaddo writers have included James Baldwin, Truman Capote, Langston Hughes, Sylvia Plath, and David Foster Wallace. Residents are housed both in the mansion and in outbuildings, most of these being cabins, but also including a stone tower beside a moss-filled pond. Yaddo is near enough to the Saratoga Race Course that in August you hear the sound of the crowd crescendoing to a roar at the end of every horse race.

And there is another race between MacDowell and Yaddo when it comes to awards received by former residents. At last count, MacDowell writers have won eighty-six Pulitzer Prizes and thirty-one National Book Awards, while Yaddo has racked up seventy-eight Pulitzer Prizes, sixty-nine National Book Awards, and a Nobel Prize (Saul Bellow). But both are open to all creatives, once you have been accepted by their panel. And of course, wherever groups of artists gather, so too will rumors of debauchery, drugs, drunkenness, and other alliterative and sometimes illicit acts, but the majority come merely to work, in privacy and peace, without the

attendant distractions of regular life. To produce. Anything else that might come along with that is a bonus.

On certain nights residents who wish to will give a presentation of their work—be it a painting displayed, or a reading, or a dance—and these are generally given a sympathetic and sophisticated audience. Both institutions are generally quieter in the winter, with fifteen or so residents dining around one long table, rather than the thirty one might find during the summer—a meeting of minds. Otherwise residents usually keep to themselves. At MacDowell your lunch is discreetly left outside your door in a picnic basket. At Yaddo you bring the lunch you are given with you to your studio in a tin lunch pail.

▲ The Frankenthaler Studio is named for painter Helen Frankenthaler's Frankenthaler Foundation, which donated substantial funds toward the cost of this new live-work studio for a visual artist. Opened in 2015, the studio is the largest of five freestanding studios at Yaddo, and it is specifically designed with the needs of contemporary artists in mind, with its retractable wall and eighteen-foot cathedral ceiling.

The long success of these two retreats has been used as a model for many others like them, including the Byrdcliffe Colony in Woodstock, New York; the Fine Arts Work Center in Provincetown, Massachusetts; the Virginia Center for the Creative Arts in Amherst, Virginia; and the Tyrone Guthrie Centre in Annaghmakerrig, Ireland.

William Faulkner

Born: September 25, 1897, New Albany, Mississippi
Died: July 6, 1962, Byhalia, Mississippi

**624 Pirate's Alley,
New Orleans, Louisiana**

This Greek Revival-style house was built in 1840 for a wealthy sugar planter in the Creole tradition, with arches on the ground floor to allow for commercial occupancy and a narrow side passageway leading to a courtyard. Pirate's Alley is one of two that flank St. Louis Cathedral.

> "If I had not existed, someone else would have written me, Hemingway, Dostoevsky, all of us."
>
> —William Faulkner

It was late 1924, and William Faulkner was heading to Europe—just as soon as his first book was published, a collection of poems called *The Marble Faun*. While he waited, a friend suggested he visit New Orleans. The timing was good, as he had just been forced to resign from his job as postmaster in Oxford, Mississippi, where he was raised, so he had ample time. In New Orleans, he met the author Sherwood Anderson, whose wife Faulkner had worked with at a New York bookshop. Anderson, two decades Faulkner's senior, lived on Jackson Square, in the French Quarter, and the two quickly became friends, drinking and discussing literature.

Anderson and his wife extended an open invitation to Faulkner to stay with them and, as Anderson would be away from the city for a time, in January 1925 Faulkner took them up on their offer. After Anderson returned to the city in March, Faulkner, having perhaps outstayed his welcome, moved in with the artist and silver designer William Spratling in his French Quarter home on the first floor of 624 Pirate's Alley (known then as "Orleans Alley South"). The house was built on the site of an eighteenth-century structure that had been the residence of the attorney general of the Superior Council of the French colony of Louisiana, as well as the yard of the French colonial prison.

For the first (and, it would turn out, the last) time, Faulkner found himself living in a city replete with creative people whose ambition (almost) equaled his own. Oxford was small, predictable, and conservative. New Orleans was—the opposite. Faulkner pivoted from poetry to prose, writing sketches for the *Times-Picayune*, New Orleans' main newspaper, and for *The Double Dealer*, the preeminent, avant-garde literary journal based in the city, which acted as a magnet for literary talent on the level to which Faulkner strived.

Faulkner wrote furiously, with twenty pieces appearing in the two publications during the first nine months of 1925. Meanwhile, in late February he started a novel, *Soldiers' Pay*, which he finished by mid-May. His encounters with the French Quarter's plentiful eccentrics provided fodder for a wide cast of characters in his fiction, allowing him finally to write about people other than himself—or, as he did in *Soldiers' Pay*, to convert into fiction the fabricated autobiographical stories he'd been spinning all along.

During the day, he worked at odd jobs in the neighborhood, or just sat and watched the parade of nuns, priests, and choirboys leaving the nearby cathedral. At night, he wrote at his desk, puffing on his pipe.

The dream of a life among creative equals was short-lived. With Anderson's encouragement, he sent *Soldiers' Pay* to a publisher, who accepted it. His destiny set in motion, Faulkner made his much-delayed trip to Europe, sailing in August. Not long after his return to the United States, Oxford—where he would write what are now regarded to be his greatest books—beckoned him back.

Maya Angelou

Born: April 4, 1928, St. Louis, Missouri
Died: May 28, 2014, Winston-Salem, North Carolina

Hotel room, Anywhere

Amid a raucous life, full of travel and
conversation and beauty and horror and
activism and music and lectures and theater
and pain and color and joy, Angelou found
the quiet anonymity of a hotel room to be
conducive to conjuring literature from
experience. And the sherry was nice too.
She described writing in hotel rooms as
being lonely and marvelous.

> "You can't use up creativity.
> The more you use, the more you have."
>
> —Maya Angelou

Maya Angelou liked to keep her house pretty. And she couldn't write surrounded by pretty. It was for this reason that, in every town she lived in, whenever she found herself ready to write, she rented a hotel room for a few months. Her routine went something like this: she rose at five-thirty or so, left home at six, and tried to be at work by six-thirty. No one was allowed entry into the room. Before she arrived, the hotel staff would have been given instructions only to empty the wastebaskets, and not to change the bedsheets, as she never slept in the room. The management might slip a note under her door pleading to change the sheets, for fear that they might be moldy, but the request would be denied. She also insisted that the room be stripped of any distracting decorations—no artwork, no flowers. On the bedside table was a dictionary, a thesaurus, a Bible, books of poetry, a yellow notepad, ballpoint pens, a deck of cards, an ashtray, a glass, and a bottle of sherry.

Angelou would read through one of the books in order to get a feel for some rhythm that might spark words, to remind herself of language, from Psalms, or poetry—maybe James Weldon Johnson or Paul Laurence Dunbar. Then, once she had found momentum, she began the labor of writing. Angelou wrote lying across the made-up bed, working for such long periods in this position that her elbow became rough with calluses. If stuck, she played solitaire to loosen the brain—to help her, as she put it, find a place of enchantment, so that she might be granted easier access to her memories. She might have her first sip of sherry as early as six-fifteen, as soon as she arrived, but generally she waited until about eleven.

Usually, she wrote until the early afternoon, hoping to have produced by then ten or twelve pages. She then went home, took a shower, and tried to forget about writing. She might go to the grocery store and pretend to be normal. At five in the afternoon she read through whatever she had written, and began the process of editing it, boiling the material down to three or four pages. Afterwards she prepared dinner, lit candles, put on music, entertained, bid farewell, cleared the dishes, and, before bed, read once more what she had written. The next morning she started it all over again, etcetera, until the thing was finished.

This method worked well for her first book, the 1969 memoir *I Know Why the Caged Bird Sings*, which has never been out of print, and so she continued this method for everything she wrote thereafter, including six subsequent autobiographies, five essay collections, numerous plays and screenplays, and the poem she was asked to write for Bill Clinton's presidential inauguration in January 1993, "On the Pulse of Morning," making her the first poet to read at a presidential inauguration since Robert Frost read at John F. Kennedy's in 1961.

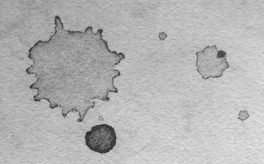

Alone in
the Crowd

Simone de Beauvoir and Jean-Paul Sartre

Born: January 9, 1908, and June 21, 1905, Paris, France
Died: April 14, 1986, and April 15, 1980, Paris, France

Les Deux Magots and Café de Flore, Paris, France

The Art Deco interior of Les Deux Magots, with its chandeliers, columns, banquettes, and brass, is reflected in wall-length mirrors. Although the Café de Flore lacked Les Deux Magots's prime corner location, its upper-floor room, often reserved for the literati, made it keen competition. In the 1940s, though, Beauvoir and Sartre saw no need to play favorites, happily splitting their time working between the two.

"I wish that every human life might be pure transparent freedom."

—Simone de Beauvoir

Simone de Beauvoir and Jean-Paul Sartre met in 1929 at Paris's École normale supérieure, an elite graduate school, where they were both candidates for the *agrégation*, the highly competitive examinations for entry into the French civil service. The school's jury, after much deliberation, gave first place to Sartre over Beauvoir—although, notably, Sartre had failed in his first attempt, and Beauvoir was the youngest person ever to pass the test. From that moment on they were intrinsically linked by competition, companionship, and erudition. It also marked the beginning of a fifty-one-year romantic relationship.

The two philosopher-authors had been immediately drawn to one another, realizing a mutual respect for one another's intellect and a shared disrespect for bourgeois norms. Instigated by Sartre, they entered a pact wherein they would never marry, though they would remain bound together. In this pact they also would be allowed to have relationships with other people, but only so long as they told each other everything. Their radical relationship formed a kind of foundation myth for mid-twentieth-century existentialism, creating a subculture that was decisively anchored in the area surrounding the Saint-Germain-des-Prés church, within Paris's Rive Gauche (Left Bank), with its many bookstores and publishing houses, and its history of nonconformism.

Sartre and Beauvoir spent several years staying in cheap Saint-Germain hotels (in separate rooms, of course) and writing all day in cafés, often just to have a place to stay warm. Before the war, weather allowing, they also frequented the tables outside. Both authors liked writing amid the clatter of public spaces. They held court at these tables with writers, artists, and students, talking over one another and smoking ceaselessly. It was all about seeing and being seen. And after the cafés, there were underground jazz bars to haunt.

Of all the cafés on offer, they favored Les Deux Magots and the Café de Flore, thirty yards apart from one another, separated only by the narrow rue Saint-Benoît, centered around the corner of boulevard Saint-Germain and rue Bonaparte. The two cafés—always in competition, operating within the same milieu but after their own distinct fashion—are fittingly symbolic of the two writers.

Les Deux Magots, which opened in 1885, inherited its name from the fabric and novelty shop previously on the premises, which itself was named after a popular play from the early 1800s. The café also inherited from the shop the two roughly life-sized statues perched high on its square central pillar. These are variously described as representing merchants or alchemists, but for the purposes of this book we will accept the theory that they depict philosophers, peering down from their adjoining corner at the same scene from perpendicular angles.

The tables beneath Les Deux Magots's large green awning have served as proving grounds for several literary and artistic movements. In its early days, the Symbolist poets, including Arthur Rimbaud, were regulars, and the café quickly became a magnet for well-known creative types, along with those who longed to join their ranks. Oscar Wilde, who lived and died just minutes away, on the rue des Beaux-Arts, was another patron. In the 1920s, James Joyce and Ernest Hemingway drank dry sherry here, and when the drunken Joyce picked fights, he would hide behind Hemingway and yell, "Deal with him, Hemingway. Deal with him." André Breton and the Surrealists created their manifesto here, thus attracting other artists, such as Man Ray and Joan Miró. Pablo Picasso discovered his lover and muse, Dora Maar, at Les Deux Magots, jabbing at the table between her fingers with a penknife.

The Café de Flore, which opened for business in the same era as Les Deux Magots, got its name from a statue of Flora, the Roman goddess of spring, that once stood opposite it on boulevard Saint-Germain. It proved to be as much a draw for writers as its competitor down the street. Samuel Beckett lived on the opposite side of the Jardin du Luxembourg, and in the decade before World War II he was often seen at a table, occasionally sitting with Joyce's son Giorgio. In the early 1950s, James Baldwin wrote much of his first novel, *Go Tell It on the Mountain*, at the Flore.

Of the two cafés, the Flore often won out, as its owner let Beauvoir and Sartre work in a private room upstairs. This privacy became more important after the end of World War II, when fame consumed Beauvoir and Sartre, and the presence of journalists and hangers-on made working at the outdoor tables unfeasible. And the Flore had another advantage, in that its upper floor had heat. Beauvoir and Sartre often sat at separate tables near the fire while, for example, Beauvoir wrote *She Came to Stay* (1943) and Sartre worked on *Being and Nothingness* (1943). Meanwhile, Albert Camus sat as far from Sartre as possible, as the writers detested each other.

In May 1946, Sartre moved in with his mother, who had a fourth-floor apartment on rue Bonaparte, on the corner of place Saint-Germain-des-Prés. Sartre's large study looked across the cobblestone square to the church and onto the terrace of Les Deux Magots, as well as the Café de Flore beyond. After fifteen years of shabby hotels, he was suddenly living like the bourgeoisie. At around one in the afternoon, if not actively in pursuit of another woman, he typically would head off for lunch with Beauvoir (who would have spent the quieter mornings writing at Les Deux Magots), then back later in the afternoon, often with Beauvoir, who would work at a small bridge table. Sartre might sit at his piano to play a Bach prelude or a Beethoven sonata, then set to work—effectively recreating the café atmosphere at home. They worked till eight in the evening, after which they would head back out into the night, perhaps dining at Brasserie Lipp, a restaurant directly across the road from the Flore and Deux Magots, which also had been in operation since the 1880s.

In the intervening years, place Saint-Germain, the cobbled square with Les Deux Magots on one corner and Sartre's former apartment at 42 rue Bonaparte on another, has been renamed place Sartre-Beauvoir.

Allen Ginsberg

Born: June 3, 1926, Newark, New Jersey
Died: April 5, 1997, New York City

Having taken peyote one October evening in 1954, Allen Ginsberg looked out the window of the apartment he shared with his girlfriend. There, through the cable car-clanging San Francisco fog, rose the Sir Francis Drake Hotel, transformed into what Ginsberg described in a letter to Jack Kerouac as a Golgotha-robot (Golgotha being the skull-shaped rock at the site of Jesus's crucifixion). Upon later reflection, this vision would transform again, into a Moloch (a child-devouring god), forming the basis for Part II of his best-known work, the long-form poem *Howl* (1956).

But not yet. First, he had to change his life completely.

Ginsberg had a job in market research, a girlfriend, an apartment in an affluent neighborhood—so why wasn't he happy? He started to see a therapist, and told him that he never wanted to work again, that he wanted to be with men, and that he wanted to live the life of a poet. To which his therapist asked, "Well, why don't you?"

1010 Montgomery Street, San Francisco, California

Kerouac was credited for naming Ginsberg's controversial poem, but Peter Orlovsky later suggested that Ginsberg may have picked it up during a moonlit walk they took together one night, when Orlovsky sang the Hank Williams tune "Howlin' at the Moon." The infamous first reading of *Howl* can be seen as the opening salvo of the cultural revolution that raged into the 1960s (and beyond).

ALONE IN THE CROWD

> "The only thing that can save the world is the reclaiming of the awareness of the world. That's what poetry does."
>
> —Allen Ginsberg

That was all it took. Ginsberg told his girlfriend he preferred men and moved out of their Nob Hill apartment and into an apartment with a painter, Robert LaVigne, and his model and lover, a young poet named Peter Orlovsky. This arrangement became awkward, however, when it grew clear that Ginsberg and Orlovsky were in love with one another. By March, Ginsberg and Orlovsky had moved into 1010 Montgomery Street, in the bohemian district of North Beach, in the northeast corner of San Francisco.

Next Ginsberg rid himself of work, by writing an apparently effective report demonstrating how his job could be replaced by an "IBM mechanical brain"—and, thus fired, his transformation was complete. He could now devote himself to writing, thinking, and communing with friends, among whom was the main Beat muse Neal Cassady, who had left his wife and now spent much of his time at Montgomery Street, bringing with him his new girlfriend and playing chess incessantly in the bay window.

Ginsberg decked out the apartment in Turkish rugs, a cushy armchair for reading, and a Webcor Victrola three-speed record player bought from a pawnshop, on which he played Bach's Mass in B Minor to serenade himself into sleep. The apartment had a fireplace to banish the chill of foggy days, and was a five-minute walk from City Lights Bookstore, which had been opened by the poet Lawrence Ferlinghetti two years previously and had already developed a reputation as a hub for radical literary ideation.

Ginsberg spent his new-found freedom drinking coffee and smoking cigarettes in Foster's Cafeteria on Montgomery Street, climbing Telegraph Hill, and reading, reading, reading: D.H. Lawrence poems, Aldous Huxley's *Doors of Perception* (1954), books on Buddhism, Herman Hesse's *Siddharta* (1922), the poetry of William Carlos Williams (who visited him in San Francisco, Ginsberg reporting him looking old and sick). Ginsberg also expended great effort in promoting the work of his fellow Beats, particularly Jack Kerouac and William Burroughs. But he didn't write that much at first; for that he needed isolation. By mid-March of that year, he was shunning everyone except Cassady and Orlovsky, so that he could focus his attention on composition.

Although he took notes in cafés, he did the meat of his writing at his desk in the apartment, gazing out the window at San Francisco's not un-Moloch-like financial district, awaiting inspiration, armed with a secondhand typewriter and a stack of blank paper. He often wrote through the night, accompanied by the sounds of the city. And Ginsberg was

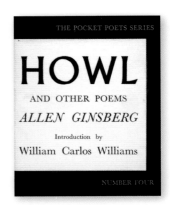

THE POCKET POETS SERIES

HOWL
AND OTHER POEMS
ALLEN GINSBERG
Introduction by
William Carlos Williams

NUMBER FOUR

▲ Published by Lawrence Ferlinghetti's San Francisco-based City Lights Press in 1956, *Howl* is referred to by the press as "the prophetic book that launched the Beat Generation." City Lights published other key Beat writers, including Ferlinghetti himself, Michael McClure, Gregory Corso, Diane di Prima, William Burroughs, Paul Bowles, Neal Cassady, and later works by Jack Kerouac and Ginsberg.

> "Fortunately art is a community effort – a small but select community living in a spiritualized world endeavoring to interpret the wars and the solitudes of the flesh."

—Allen Ginsberg

a poet powered by sound. He knew the poem he wanted to write needed to work as a spoken piece, a text for a performance, a vessel for public consumption. He envisioned himself reading aloud, addressing an audience that would include his closest literary companions, specifically Cassady and Kerouac.

Soon he had hit upon the idea of a poem that would consist of a long series of stanzas that could be read in single-breath bursts, in an incantatory fashion. His working title for the poem was "Strophes," in reference to Greek choral poetry. And, although the poem was inspired in part by a drug-induced vision, Ginsberg tended to write sober (unlike some of his Beat contemporaries). He did write in a kind of trance, though, letting his imagination lead him wherever it would, and only revising afterwards.

By the middle of 1955, he had grown worried about the financial straits his new life had left him in. On the allotted day he would leave his apartment at eight in the morning and sit in a park waiting for the unemployment office to open, watching people pass. He started to encourage Kerouac to move to San Francisco, telling him that, after he finished his poem, they could "go down and conquer Hollywood." But in mid-August he wrote to Kerouac again, saying he was more absorbed in his writing than ever, and enclosing a first draft of the poem, which was now entitled *Howl*. Kerouac wrote back, saying the poem was very powerful, and that he needed to make sure not to edit out its original power.

At the end of August, Ginsberg wrote to Kerouac to report that City Lights were to publish *Howl* as a stand-alone fifty-page pamphlet. He continued to insist that Kerouac join him out west, but now in Berkeley, across the bay from San Francisco, where he had found a cottage for thirty-five dollars a month, as he would only be in the Montgomery Street apartment another few weeks. He also politely requested that Kerouac, who was in Mexico, pick up some mescaline and bring it with him.

Ginsberg moved into his cottage in Berkeley on September 1, 1955. Kerouac joined him there later that month, and began his attempts, in vain, to prevent Ginsberg from editing his poem. On the night of October 7, Kerouac and Ginsberg caught a bus into San Francisco, then caught a lift with Ferlinghetti to the Six Gallery, where *Howl* was first performed. A drunken Kerouac sat to the side of the stage, shouting "Yeah! Go!" at the end of certain stanzas. After the reading, Cassady passed around a collection plate.

J. D. Salinger

Born: January 1, 1919, New York City
Died: January 27, 2010, Cornish, New Hampshire

The Beekman Tower hotel,
3 Mitchell Place, New York City

Salinger booked a two-week stay in the Beekman with an aim to finish a story he had been ruminating on for almost a year, about a young man, sick of preparatory school and wanting to "get the hell out of New York." The story ends with the teary-eyed narrator waiting for a bus on Madison Avenue, a few blocks from the hotel.

> "I write for myself, for my own pleasure.
> And I want to be left alone to do it."
>
> —J. D. Salinger

In early 1941, twenty-two-year-old J. D. Salinger was feeling broke, so he took employment as entertainment director on board the SS *Kungsholm*, an Art Deco cruise ship, and in mid-February, the liner set sail from New York Harbor for the Caribbean. But with the war in Europe beginning to ramp up in earnest, Salinger soon felt he was wasting his time accompanying the daughters of passengers to dances and organizing deck sports, and he left the ship a few weeks later. (It was also to be the *Kungsholm*'s last pleasure voyage, as it was requisitioned by the navy in December of that year.)

Not long afterward, he tried to enlist in the army but was rejected due to an irregularity of the heart. In July, he went on holiday to the New Jersey shore, at the house of a military school friend, whose sister introduced him to a set of wealthy young women, including Gloria Vanderbilt and a sixteen-year-old Oona O'Neill (daughter of the playwright Eugene O'Neill), with whom Salinger was briefly romantically involved. In August, Salinger returned to New York, where, perhaps finding it hard to write in the apartment he shared with his parents, he rented a room for two weeks in the Beekman Tower hotel.

When this twenty-six-story Art Deco skyscraper opened at the corner of First Avenue and East 49th Street in Midtown Manhattan, in October 1928, it was known as the Panhellenic Tower, as it initially only accepted women in sororities as guests. It was one of only five hotels in New York City to avoid bankruptcy during the Great Depression, and to stay afloat it started accepting men in the mid-1930s, changing its name to the Beekman Tower to reflect this change. (After James Beekman, who on the site in 1765 built a mansion, which during the Revolutionary War was taken over by the British, who tried Nathan Hale for espionage in the house's garden and hanged him in its orchard.) The tower featured a rooftop solarium that by 1940 had become "The Top of the Tower," a popular cocktail lounge.

Salinger later complained that his time at the Beekman had been unproductive, but he was able to finish a story entitled "The Lovely Dead Girl at Table Six," which he had been working on for a year. After leaving the Beekman, he sent the story to his agent, receiving a lukewarm response. But in October 1941 he received the news he'd long been awaiting: his story, since retitled "Slight Rebellion off Madison," had been bought by the *New Yorker*. Publication was planned for its December issue, to match the month in which the story was set. But after the Japanese bombed Pearl Harbor on December 7, the magazine suspended publication indefinitely. The tone just no longer fit the national mood.

Salinger was drafted into the army in 1942, and fought during the 1944 D-Day landings at Normandy. The story, finally published by the *New Yorker* in December 1946, later served as the basis for his novel *Catcher in the Rye* (1951).

"People give pain, are callous and insensitive, empty and cruel . . . but place heals the hurt, soothes the outrage, fills the terrible vacuum that these human beings make."

—Eudora Welty

"Walking into the crowd was like sinking into a stew—you became an ingredient, you took on a certain flavour."

—Margaret Atwood

"The time when, most of all, you should withdraw into yourself is when you are forced to be in a crowd."

—Epicurus

"In Heaven an angel is nobody in particular."

—George Bernard Shaw

J. K. Rowling

Born: July 31, 1965, Yate, UK

Café Majestic, Rua de Santa Catarina, Porto, Portugal

When you write the best-selling book series of all time, people want to know where the magic happened. The truth is complex, and so is Café Majestic, one of the many cafés in which Rowling wrote her first Harry Potter book. Old world opulence, formality mixed with levity, very strong coffee—did it inspire the Harryverse? Finding out is a Muggle's game.

"No story lives unless someone wants to listen."

—J. K. Rowling

It was the summer of 1990. J. K. Rowling was on a train. She had spent the weekend apartment hunting with her boyfriend in Manchester, and was on her way home to London. The train was delayed, and as she waited, an idea came to her, unbidden, about a series of books regaling the adventures of a boy in a school for wizards. The idea gripped her. She knew she had to write it. So she started, putting pen to paper in her flat above a sports shop in Clapham Junction. Six months later, her world was thrown into disarray when her mother died. She was devastated, and at a loss for what to do. For three years she had bounced from one unsatisfactory job to another, been frustrated in her attempts at writing a novel, and then a second novel, and now her relationship had ended. She needed a new direction.

This new direction came when she took a position at the Encounter School in Porto, Portugal, teaching English as a foreign language. When she first arrived, she shared a flat above a drugstore with two other women who taught at the school. Their lessons were from five to ten on weeknights, and after class they would often head out to nightclubs, but even with late nights she was still left with plenty of time to write during the day. To write she needed coffee, and in Porto there was no finer place to have coffee than the Belle Époque-era Café Majestic on Rua de Santa Catarina.

The Majestic, with its aroma of leather upholstery and bitter coffee, and its gloss of varnished wood duplicated in multiple Flemish mirrors, is heavy with metal and marble, and light with stained glass and plaster statues of laughing fauns. Among the general café clatter she wrote, perhaps snacking on *pastéis de nata*, a Portuguese pastry tart, with pen in notepads (not on café napkins, as was later claimed). Later she would type up her notes in the Encounter School, before her classes began. And Porto's evocative setting likely contributed to the *mise-en-scène* she was in the midst of creating: narrow, winding, steep cobbled streets, blind alleyways, mist rising off the Douro River past grand, regal buildings, mysterious and crumbling. Some things certainly leaked through: Rowling later confirmed that Portugal's decades-long dictator, António Salazar, lent his name to the shadowy Salazar Slytherin.

After eighteen months in Porto, Rowling met a Portuguese journalism student who shared her love of Jane Austen. They married in October 1992, and in July 1993, they had a daughter, whom they named after the author Jessica Mitford. The marriage, turbulent from the beginning, soon came to a crisis point, and it was over by November. When Rowling headed with her baby to Edinburgh that December, she had three finished chapters in her suitcase. Spoiler alert: things worked out well for her. The first book in the series, *Harry Potter and the Philosopher's Stone*, was published in 1997, and in 2015, *Forbes* named her the world's first billionaire author.

Residencies

From a beach house on the Gulf of Mexico to a medieval Italian castle with
fragrant gardens, a cattle ranch to an ancient forest, residencies have one aim:
to remove the distractions of quotidian routine, to allow the artist to focus
the mind on the essence of creativity.

There is often as much competition for entry into residencies as for entry into some of the more established retreats, but many of them also offer free accommodation or even stipends, so that attendees can concentrate on work without worrying about paying the bills back home. Which is good, because, except for the lucky and/or talented few, writers are generally an impoverished lot, meaning most are happy to rely, occasionally, on the kindness of strangers. But, of course, if you picked this book up in the middle of a pandemic, such as the one it was written in, this section may read as fiction—a list of places as fantastical and out of reach as Lilliput and Blefuscu. Be that as it may, find here a cursory introduction to the wonderful world of residencies.

If you want to benefit by osmosis from the aura of a writer's former home, there's the Kerouac Project, which gives four writers a year the chance to work for three months in the cottage where Jack Kerouac wrote his novel *Dharma Bums*, in Orlando, Florida, with only two formal obligations—a welcome potluck dinner and a final reading. Or, if it's grandiosity you're after, you can try for a residency in the seventeenth-century poet William Drummond's former home—a Scottish castle south of Edinburgh on a clifftop overlooking the River North Esk, with a tower that dates from the fourteenth century (applications by mail only). There's also the Civitella Ranieri Foundation, which hosts six-week residencies for twelve to fourteen people in a fifteenth-century castle in rural central Italy, amidst gardens of roses and lavender.

Indeed, most residencies lean toward the pastoral.

The Vermont Studio Center, the largest residency program in the United States, houses up to fifty-two artists and writers in a series of buildings along the Gihon River in the village of Johnson, in the Green Mountains. The chosen few can also stay in the Hermitage Artist Retreat's beach house on a four-hundred-foot-wide sandbar on Florida's Gulf Coast, south of Tampa. At certain times of the year, residents here are required to keep their curtains tightly closed at night to prevent light from leaking and diverting baby sea turtles from their intended path.

Remoteness is also common. The Jentel Artist Residency Program takes place on a thousand-acre working cattle

▲ Civitella Ranieri Castle. The Civitella Ranieri Foundation invites from twelve to fourteen writers, composers, and visual artists to each of the four six-week self-directed residencies offered every year. Author Rachel Kushner finished her acclaimed novel *The Mars Room* (2018) at the castle, calling it "an exquisite place to work."

ranch in Wyoming, with views over scoria-capped hills leading up to the Bighorn Mountains. There are few signs of human existence along the two-mile stretch of Piney Creek that flows through the property, which includes two writer studios in a log cabin. Then there's the Fish Factory Creative Centre in Stöðvarfjörður, a remote village in the eastern fjords of Iceland. (They also host a fish-processing company and the local fish market—a far remove from roses and lavender.)

For the rugged writer, there's the ten-day Artist-in-Residence Program in Denali National Park, Alaska, which gives writers time alone (very alone) in a ranger patrol cabin. And writers with an eye on eternity might consider immersing themselves in an ancient forest for a few weeks, through the Andrews Forest Writers Residency—part of an Oregon State University program that aims to create a two-hundred-year record of human–sylvan interactions.

▲ Stöðvarfjörður Harbor, Iceland—home of the Fish Factory Creative Centre on the isolated east coast of the island, which offers residencies in a range of fields, from textile art, music, and literature to sustainable design, engineering, photography, and more. Selected applicants pay a fee for accommodation and use of the facilities, including studio and/or workshop space. Iceland is dark and peaceful for much of the winter—perfect for thinking (and sleeping)!

And then there are the residencies with no fixed location—or rather, a location in constant flux. Amtrak's Residency for Writers gives two writers a month a round-trip journey on any of their fifteen long-distance routes. Then there's the Arctic Circle, an annual "expeditionary" residency program, which brings artists together with scientists to explore the Svalbard Archipelago far north of Scandinavia in the Arctic Ocean on a schooner barque sailing vessel. Bring writing mittens.

Willa Cather

Born: December 7, 1873, Gore, Virginia
Died: April 24, 1947, New York City

In 1912, Willa Cather moved to an apartment at 5 Bank Street in Greenwich Village with Edith Lewis, who lived with Cather from 1908 until the author's death. The Village originally took shape in 1798 when an outbreak of yellow fever spurred the Bank of New York to flee Wall Street, with other banks following suit after further epidemics, largely settling along what eventually became Bank Street. The writers who were Cather's fellow Greenwich Village residents were the canon of the time: John Dos Passos, Theodore Dreiser, Sinclair Lewis, e e cummings, Robert Frost. It was a long way from Red Cloud, Nebraska, where Cather had spent her formative years.

5 Bank Street,
Greenwich Village, New York City
Rent when Cather and Lewis moved in was forty-two dollars a month, though afterwards this doubled, then tripled (a familiar story for New Yorkers). They furnished the apartment with a mahogany table and chests bought from an auction room, large Oriental rugs, and low, open bookshelves. Cather hung the walls with reproductions of Old Masters and an etching of George Sand. Despite the profusion of literary social events, the two women preferred the opera.

Garden
Domain

George Bernard Shaw

Born: July 26, 1856, Dublin, Ireland
Died: November 2, 1950, Ayot St. Lawrence, UK

The rotating shed at Shaw's Corner, Ayot St. Lawrence, UK

George Bernard Shaw sought to obliterate boundaries, to test the lines between the public and the private, the internal and the external. This shed, unfixed, dramatic, and subtly located in a pocket of greenery on the edge of an expansive, cultivated garden, acted as a fitting symbol of, and vessel for, the productive last forty-four years of his life.

"The worst sin towards our fellow creatures
is not to hate them, but to be indifferent
to them: that's the essence of inhumanity."

—George Bernard Shaw

In 1906, after a long search for a home, George Bernard Shaw—playwright, socialist, feminist, vegetarian, and eventual Nobel Prize winner—discovered a recently built rectory in Ayot St. Lawrence, a small village twenty miles north of London. Shaw said it was the silence and stillness of the house and gardens that attracted him to the property, which eventually gained the name "Shaw's Corner." He and his wife would live there for the rest of their lives. Although the house was rather grand, as befitted a man of Shaw's fame and standing, Shaw preferred to do his writing in a shed, thought to have been purchased as a kit at some point in the 1920s and installed in the extensive gardens.

Shaw nicknamed the shed "London" so that people who dropped by could be told that he was working in the capital—a cunning method of keeping visitors at bay. He found that people distracted him, and his retreat among the trees enabled him to escape from the press of humanity. This isolation was helped by the fact that the shed was hidden behind a patch of mature trees in an area of near wilderness, and accessed by crossing the perfectly laid lawns, then walking down the entire length of the garden. It was built onto a platform with casters, so that Shaw could turn it, with just a push of the shoulder, to follow the sun throughout the day. He preferred working in natural light, and the sun on the windows provided warmth. In the winter months, the trees gave shelter, and the shed could be turned to face them. Shaw said that, when writing, he saw the future performance playing out in his head. Being able to look out onto his own personal theater space—his garden—made the shed a perfect place for creativity. Ever the showman, he also was savvy enough to present the shed as an advertisement for some of his dearly held ideals, such as health reform and the draw of the socialist lifestyle (contradicted though that might have been by the opulence of the house).

Although only eight feet square, the shed held all Shaw needed for his work. Besides his desk and cane chair, there was a bunk for resting—essential for any serious writer, and even more so for one who wrote plays at what he described as "a helter-skelter pace." If the sun didn't shine (a fairly likely proposition in middle England), he also had a kerosene heater and an electric light, and a telephone intercom linked to the house, so that he could call his staff for refreshments. Everything was within arm's reach; his typewriter could be pulled from the shelf under the bunk without having to move from his chair. Shaw felt that stepping outside and taking a short break in the air to rotate the shed was good for his health, and he must have been right, as he continued to write in the shed up to his death at the age of ninety-four.

Virginia Woolf

Born: January 25, 1882, London
Died: March 28, 1941, Lewes, UK

Writing lodge, Monk's House, Rodmell, UK

Virginia Woolf once wrote that a woman of her time who wished to write fiction required two things: a room of her own (that she could lock) and sufficient money. Her writing lodge in the gardens of Monk's House more than sufficiently provided her the first requirement. The second requirement was less of an issue for the affluent author.

received his master's on the Syracuse program, where he met his future wife, a fellow writer on the program, and he has gone back to teach the course for more than two decades. Donna Tartt, Bret Easton Ellis, and Jonathan Lethem were all classmates at Bennington College in the 1980s. The University of East Anglia (UEA), in England, which has perhaps the most storied program outside of the United States, was set up in 1970, with Ian McEwan as its first student. Angela Carter taught Anne Enright and Kazuo Ishiguro there, and W.G. Sebald taught there for three decades.

Every program has its own character. The Johns Hopkins University program is thought to be cerebral, whereas Brown University's leans experimental. Boston University's one-year program is intense. In choosing prospective students, writing programs look for not only talent and ambition, but teachability and collegiality, creating a sort of filtering system that alleviates pressure on the traditional gatekeepers of literature: editors and publishers.

▲ Dey House, home of the Iowa Writers' Workshop today. The International Writing Program is held in Shambaugh House, across the street. Early Iowa Workshop classes were held in temporary Quonset huts on the university campus; the Iowa website quotes workshop graduate Robert Dana's comments about the huts: "None of the classrooms in these huts had air conditioning . . . and when the rain drummed down on them, all talk ceased. . . . Nonetheless, the workshop quarters were basically humble." How it has all changed!

And going through a university program can fast-track the publication process. Lorrie Moore's master's thesis short stories at Cornell (where she was taught by Alison Lurie) were published soon after graduation (as *Self-Help*, in 1985). Michael Chabon received a six-figure advance for his master's thesis novel (*The Mysteries of Pittsburgh*, 1988) after his professor at UC Irvine sent it to an agent. And, of course, with hundreds of MFA creative writing programs now available in the United States alone, the competition for the number of publishing slots only grows more fierce.

Roald Dahl

Born: September 13, 1916, Llandaff, Wales, UK
Died: November 23, 1990, Oxford, UK

Writing hut at Gipsy House, Great Missenden, UK

Dahl didn't mind a filthy hut, transported as he was into his imagination whenever he was in it (though he would clean up his pet nanny goat's droppings any time she broke in). The crumpled paper, the dust, the dead leaves scattered around the floor? They could stay. Fitting for a space he referred to as a nest.

"We may enjoy our room in the tower, with the painted walls and the commodious bookcases, but down in the garden there is a man digging who buried his father this morning, and it is he and his like who live the real life and speak the real language."

—Virginia Woolf

Martin Amis

Born: August 25, 1949, Oxford, UK

Lemmons, Barnet, UK

Lemmons was a hive of literary activity,
perhaps even before Amis's family moved in.
(It is thought that Anthony Trollope's mother
may have lived there for two years in the
nineteenth century.)

> "Someone watches over us when we write.
> Mother. Teacher. Shakespeare. God."
>
> —Martin Amis

It was April 1972. Cecil Day-Lewis, the Poet Laureate of the United Kingdom, was gravely ill. The novelist Elizabeth Jane Howard (who had had a brief affair with Day-Lewis in the 1950s, while friends with his wife, the actor Jill Balcon) wanted to help. And so she invited Day-Lewis—along with Balcon and their two children, Tamasin and Daniel—to stay with her at Lemmons, the home she shared with her husband, the novelist Kingsley Amis.

Lemmons (or Gladsmuir House, as it was known before Howard changed its name) was a two-story, twenty-room Georgian villa built in 1830 on the outskirts of north London, on eight acres of land that included a rose garden, a conservatory, and a detached cottage for a housekeeper. There was evidently plenty of room at the house, even though Howard's mother (a former ballerina) and brother (nicknamed "Monkey") lived there as well, as did a painter named Sargy Mann. Kingsley's three children from his previous marriage were also often in residence. One of them, his son Martin, had recently graduated from Oxford University and taken a job with the *Times Literary Supplement*, necessitating a move to London. But the draw of Lemmons remained strong, and he would return on the weekends.

Lemmons was always busy with visitors during the family's eight years in the house, particularly writers (and writers-to-be). These included John Betjeman, Iris Murdoch, Philip Larkin, Elizabeth Bowen, and Martin's friends Christopher Hitchens and Julian Barnes. Howard and Kingsley wrote two novels each while living at Lemmons, and it was Howard (rather than Kingsley) who had first encouraged Martin to start reading literature, directing him initially toward Jane Austen.

In his 2000 memoir *Experience*, Martin Amis wrote that every weekend at Lemmons was a "citadel of riotous insolvency," with his father as "the hub of all humour and high spirits, like an engine of comedy." And, to be sure, the drink flowed freely. (Kingsley wrote for *Playboy* magazine, which regularly sent him free liquor.) Amis also wrote of the security he felt when at Lemmons, and the subsequent insecurity whenever he left it to join the uncertain world. He hadn't yet made a name for himself—hadn't yet separated his identity from that of his titan of a father—but this was soon to change. In July 1970, in his bedroom above his father's study, Amis had started the first draft of his first novel, *The Rachel Papers*. Literary renown (and, some would say, infamy) would come his way. But not quite yet.

The Amis/Howard and Day-Lewis families had been close for a long time, so they mixed naturally. Tamasin and Martin had a brief relationship that ended gradually and amicably. She understood that, for Amis, writing, drinking, and male friends came first. She also later wrote that she had conspired with Howard, who was her godmother, to bring her family to Lemmons when her father fell sick. He died five weeks after they moved in, shortly after writing his final poem, entitled "At Lemmons."

The Solace
of Nature

Anton Chekhov

Born: January 29, 1860, Taganrog, Russia
Died: July 15, 1904, Badenweiler, Germany

The cottage at Melikhovo, Russia

"Melikhovo is a healthy place; it stands exactly on a watershed, on high ground, so that there is never fever or diphtheria in it," Chekhov wrote to A. S. Suvorin. He lived here contentedly until 1897, when his worsening tuberculosis instigated a move to sunnier climes. Some of the linden and birch trees Chekhov planted still grow today, and a nearby town was christened "Chekhov" in 1954.

> **"Man will become better when you show him what he is like."**
>
> —Anton Chekhov

Anton Chekhov was exhausted. It was late autumn, 1891, and the thirty-one-year-old had recently returned to his home in Moscow from a grueling, year-long journey gathering information for a census on the dire circumstances of the prisoners at Sakhalin Island, a Russian penal colony to the north of Japan. He was feeling stultified by the literary life in Moscow, and was looking to broaden his horizons. As he wrote in a letter to A. S. Suvorin, a journalist, publisher, and longtime friend, "If I am a doctor I ought to have patients and a hospital; if I am a literary man I ought to live among people instead of in a flat with a mongoose [referring to his pet mongoose, Svoloch ("bastard" in Russian)] . . . this life between four walls, without nature, without people, without a country, without health and appetite, is not life."

Chekhov—now considered to be a master of both short stories and plays—had already found literary success, and this apart from his work as a physician (another reason for his exhaustion). But he felt drawn to the countryside, and in early 1892 he saw an advertisement for an estate of nearly 640 acres near the small town of Melikhovo, forty miles south of Moscow. He made an impulsive decision to buy it (before even visiting the property), and had soon moved there with his parents and sister. The estate's beauty only became evident after that winter's snows had finally receded. In March, he wrote, "There are avenues of lime trees, apple trees, cherries, plums, and raspberries in the garden."

Chekhov launched into repairing and restoring the previously neglected grounds, dividing tasks amongst his family members and visitors (who were legion, but welcome), seeing to the planting of trees and bulbs himself, often beginning at four in the morning in the early sun of summer. Once he had finished gardening, the industrious Chekhov typically wrote till eleven o'clock, when his mother would make him lunch. After lunch, a short nap, followed by more writing, until dinner at seven in the evening, then walks or more work in the garden, and then to bed at ten.

But these were only on days when his medical duties didn't steal him away from his adopted profession. And if patients were unable to come to him, he would travel, often a considerable distance, to minister to their needs in their own homes. Many of those he treated were impoverished peasants unable to pay for his services, and he often provided them with medicine he purchased himself, or which he created from plants grown at Melikhovo. All of this took away from writing time, though he persevered. "I am finishing a story . . . a very dull one, owing to a complete absence of woman and the element of love," he wrote to a friend in April of that year. The "dull" story in question was "Ward No. 6," a tour de force parable of the existential crisis experienced by the creative class in Russia.

A much larger distraction was on its way, however. The fifth major outbreak of cholera

"When a person is born, he can embark on only one
of three roads of life: if you go right, the
wolves will eat you; if you go left, you'll eat the
wolves; if you go straight, you'll eat yourself."

—Anton Chekhov

in the nineteenth century, which had already raged through Europe for a decade, had yet to reach Chekhov's new district. It was close, though, and finding fertile ground amongst a population already weakened by a year of famine. As he wrote to Suvorin in August 1892, "There is cholera in Moscow . . . and it will be in our parts some day soon." Chekhov was appointed cholera doctor (at no pay) in charge of twenty-six villages, and oversaw the construction of barracks in which to house the sick and dying. "Imagine my cholera-boredom," he wrote, "my cholera-loneliness, and compulsory literary inactivity."

With his cholera work finished by the end of 1893, Chekhov was able to turn his attention to writing once again—that is, when Melikhovo wasn't loud with visitors, as it often was in the summer. He would frequently disappear into his study for a few minutes at a time, to jot down a line or two as they occurred to him. Nor did his contributions to the district end with his medical practice. He also showed an interest in the education of the local populace, overseeing the construction of three schools, and donating textbooks and furniture. All of this, coupled with the fact that his study at the time doubled as his medical office, provided further barriers to writing.

To resolve this issue, Chekhov built a two-story cottage in a cherry orchard near the house in the summer of 1894. The ground floor served as the reception for his medical practice, while the floor above contained his writing desk. He soon put this innovation to good use. In October 1895, he wrote to Suvorin: "I am writing a play. . . . It's a comedy, there are three women's parts, six men's, four acts, landscapes (view over a lake); a great deal of conversation about literature, little action, tons of love." This was *The Seagull* (published in 1895), which would become his best-known work. He followed this up the next year with *Uncle Vanya* (1898) and later with some of his most enduring stories, including "Gooseberries" and "About Love." The actor Olga Knipper, whom Chekhov would later marry, stayed in the cottage for three days in 1899.

In many ways this cottage was perfect for a writer in Chekhov's situation. As a doctor, he was an integral part of the community, intrinsically tied to citizens hailing from the full spectrum of ranks and classes. As a writer, he was inherently private, sequestered. The upper floor of the cottage, with the window propped open on a warm day, air redolent of cherry blossom, put him both at a remove from and within earshot of his community—laborers tending to his estate, members of his family moving about with their daily complaints and requests, patients seeking counsel. Amidst it all was Chekhov, surrounded by joy, controversy, conversation, life, and with a fine perspective over it all.

Henry David Thoreau

Born: July 12, 1817, Concord, Massachusetts
Died: May 6, 1862, Concord, Massachusetts

What people tend to forget about Henry David Thoreau's time at Walden Pond is that, aside from informing the contents of a book—*Walden; or, Life in the Woods*—it also served as a venue in which to write another book altogether: *A Week on the Concord and Merrimack Rivers*, his first, which records a journey Thoreau undertook with his brother John in 1839, traveling via boat between two Concords (Massachusetts and New Hampshire).

In their hometown of Concord (Massachusetts), the Thoreau brothers had the previous year opened a grammar school, where they set about implementing progressive projects, particularly through an understanding of the role of humans within the natural world. These principles reflected a mindset that aligned closely with that of Ralph Waldo Emerson, the poet and philosopher with whom Thoreau had recently struck up a strong kinship. Fourteen years Thoreau's senior, Emerson quickly became a mentor and patron to the author.

Cabin at Walden Pond, Concord, Massachusetts

Everything Thoreau did during his time at Walden Pond was executed strictly through principle, by way of metaphor. The proposition taken as a whole was a form of early performance art—the acts of a deliberately lived life, carried out for the purpose of recording, disseminating, persuading, and entertaining. This pencil-maker's son is our proto-environmentalist, our advocate for just disobedience, our strident abolitionist.

THE SOLACE OF NATURE

> **"No definition of poetry is adequate unless it be poetry itself."**
>
> —Henry David Thoreau

The bond between the two authors was intensified by tragedy in January 1842, when John contracted tetanus after cutting his finger while sharpening a razor, and died in Thoreau's arms days later. Thoreau afterward went through an extended period of mourning, during which Emerson was hugely supportive, both personally and artistically. His greatest gift to Thoreau, though, was in allowing him to build a cabin beside a pond within a fourteen-acre plot of land he owned, a mile and a half from his home.

What resulted was Thoreau's great literary experiment, two years, two months, and two days in the making, from July 1845 to September 1847. A writer's relationship with a retreat is one of degrees. Some are gifted to the author, others are rented or bought. But there aren't many other examples where a retreat was built by an author from scratch. Thoreau's intention was "to build me a house which will surpass any on the main street in Concord"—surpassing in the sense of transcending. He borrowed an ax to fell trees for the cabin's frame, making sure to return the tool in better condition than he found it. He dug a six-foot-square cellar, disrupting a woodchuck burrow. And, as he wrote in *Walden*,

> Before winter I built a chimney, and shingled the sides of my house, which were already impervious to rain, with imperfect and sappy shingles made of the first slice of the log. . . . I have thus a tight shingled and plastered house, ten feet wide by fifteen long, and eight-feet posts, with a garret and a closet, a large window on each side, two trap doors, one door at the end, and a brick fireplace opposite.

After this account he itemizes the costs of every nail, latch, and hinge, giving a grand total of twenty-eight dollars, twelve and one half cents. Thus settled into his cabin, he set to writing a memorial of sorts for his brother (though he didn't once mention him by name in the book).

The interior of the cabin was kept studiously austere. Thoreau slept on a simple cot and wrote with inkstand and paper at a small green lift-top desk in the cabin—or, just as often, outside in the nature he strove to comprehend and document. On warm summer evenings he sat in the doorway and played his flute. He devoted time to scientific enquiry by, for example, crawling onto the frozen pond one winter to carry out investigations into its depth. ("It is remarkable how long men will believe in the bottomlessness of a pond without taking the trouble to sound it," he wrote.)

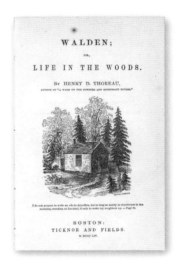

▲ *A Week on the Concord and Merrimack Rivers*, Thoreau's first book, published in 1849, featured a note announcing the imminent publication of *Walden; or, Life in the Woods.* Unfortunately, as *A Week* sold very badly, publishers were not keen to take on *Walden*, and the book wasn't published until August 1854. The two thousand copies printed were sold for a dollar per copy. The book continued to sell moderately well, and there was a marked increase in interest in the 1890s. Today, the book is regarded as a classic.

"For many years I was self-appointed inspector of snowstorms and rainstorms, and did my duty faithfully, though I never received one cent for it."

—Henry David Thoreau

He dined from the bounty of his "seven miles" of bean-rows, and from hornpout (a kind of catfish) caught from the pond, all cooked in the makeshift firepit he installed beside the cabin. "I came to love my rows, my beans, though so many more than I wanted. They attached me to the earth. . . . My enemies are worms, cool days, and most of all woodchucks. The last have nibbled for me a quarter of an acre clean"—revenge for the disrupted burrow, perhaps. His mother also often visited with food, and he would often head to Concord for dinner at the houses of friends, including Nathaniel Hawthorne and the parents of a teenage Louisa May Alcott. In the summer of 1846, he hosted at the cabin a meeting of the Concord Female Anti-Slavery Society, with speeches given in front of his doorway.

Every day was an exercise in simple ecstasy:

> After hoeing, or perhaps reading and writing, in the forenoon, I usually bathed again in the pond, swimming across one of its coves for a stint, and washed the dust of labor from my person, or smoothed out the last wrinkle which study had made, and for the afternoon was absolutely free. Every day or two I strolled to the village to hear some of the gossip which is incessantly going on there, circulating either from mouth to mouth, or from newspaper to newspaper, and which, taken in homœopathic doses, was really as refreshing in its way as the rustle of leaves and the peeping of frogs.

In modern times, Thoreau's *Walden* has come under some criticism as misrepresenting his time in the woods, the complaint being that its author was not as self-sufficient or isolated as he put forth. This misses the point. His intention was not to demonstrate his own rugged ability to survive in the wild. It was, rather, to communicate, to act as a liaison between the wider public and nature, to show that a middle ground was both possible and necessary. It was also foremost a literary project, a way of interpreting history and culture through a wider natural lens. As he wrote in *Walden*, "I think that I love society as much as most. . . . I am naturally no hermit," saying he had three chairs in his house, "one for solitude, two for friendship, three for society." The writer, for Thoreau, "speaks to the intellect and health of mankind, to all in any age who can *understand* him."

"A quiet secluded life in the country, with the possibility of being useful to people to whom it is easy to do good, and who are not accustomed to have it done to them; then work which one hopes may be of some use; then rest, nature, books, music, love for one's neighbor— such is my idea of happiness."

—Leo Tolstoy

"How vain it is to sit down to write when you have not stood up to live."

—Henry David Thoreau

"Nature knows no indecencies; man invents them."

—Mark Twain

George Orwell

Born: June 25, 1903, Motihari, Bengal (now India)
Died: January 21, 1950, London

Born into an upper-middle-class family and educated at Eton College, Orwell spent years finding out where his political empathy lay—and how to turn himself into a writer. The two quests became one. He worked as a dishwasher in Paris, lived among tramps in London, and traveled across the north of England to see firsthand the effects of poverty and unemployment on the working class. These experiences gave rise to the documentary-style *Down and Out in Paris and London* and *The Road to Wigan Pier*. But the real turning point for Orwell was the Spanish Civil War (1936–39), in which he fought on the side of the Workers' Party of Marxist Unification. From then on he avowed that every word he wrote would be written, "directly or indirectly . . . for democratic socialism, as I understand it."

Barnhill, Island of Jura, Scotland

A forty-eight-hour journey from London by train, boat, bus, taxi, and, finally, on foot, the secluded farmhouse of Barnhill on a remote island gave George Orwell the freedom and isolation he needed to write his last and most influential work, *Nineteen Eighty-Four*. Surrounded by moorland, the house consisted of a large kitchen and sitting room with four bedrooms above—one being Orwell's own, where he worked. From his window he could look across a field to Jura Sound—shimmering or stormy—and, on a fine day, the coast of Scotland. His health was so delicate by now, however, that he often lay on his bed to work, chain-smoking roll-ups of black tobacco in an atmosphere already made smoky and fetid by an inadequate grate and a kerosene stove. Completing the book meant bidding farewell to Jura for the last time and journeying south to receive the care he so badly needed.

> **"You have made an indelible mark on English literature . . . you are among the few memorable writers of your generation."**
>
> —Desmond MacCarthy to George Orwell, shortly before his death

Orwell achieved his aim most famously with the political satire *Animal Farm* (1946) and the stark warning against totalitarianism, *Nineteen Eighty-Four* (1949), his last and most celebrated novel. He wrote the latter on the remote Scottish island of Jura, which he had chosen as an escape from the demands of literary London. He was by now a successful author and journalist, and wanted to distance himself, even from friends, to accomplish a sustained piece of writing. He had also suffered a lung hemorrhage, a sign of the tuberculosis that would kill him. But he refused to admit he had the disease or seek medical help, which would have hospitalized him and prevented him from writing.

Arriving for a first visit in May 1946, Orwell took to life on Jura despite—or perhaps even because of—its lack of amenities. Barnhill, the farmhouse he rented, was seven miles from the nearest village, Ardlussa, so he acquired an unreliable motorbike and a battered van. Coal had to be transported from Ardlussa and there was little wood. The house had no telephone or electricity, and the water supply, from a tank up the hill, could run dry in the summer. But Orwell delighted in the pristine nature and the outdoor tasks of planting, chopping, digging, and carrying that such a life required. His young son Richard later remembered it as "marvellous for a child, with acres of land to roam."

Writing *Nineteen Eighty-Four* was essentially a race against time. When the second draft was finished, he felt too ill to type a fair copy himself. But no typist could be persuaded to travel to Jura with winter approaching, so he tackled the "grisly job" himself, bashing away on his old typewriter until it was finished, in November 1948. It was published the following year, captured high literary praise, and became a spectacularly successful bestseller.

Drawing on his recent memories of war-ravaged London, Orwell constructed a futuristic metropolis. Against this backdrop, the protagonist, Winston Smith, works at the Ministry of Truth on falsifying the past. The Party, headed by Big Brother, controls all thought as well as action, and Winston's love affair with a fellow worker ends in arrest, betrayal, and brainwashing. Orwell's warning about absolute power and the accompanying destruction of memory and language—and therefore logic and emotion—resonated in the postwar world, and continues to do so. The words and phrases he coined, such as "Newspeak" and "doublethink," and of course the title itself have long been part of the English language. And the dystopian nightmare he conjured up can only ever be described as . . . Orwellian.

Norman Mailer

Born: January 31, 1923, Long Branch, New Jersey
Died: November 10, 2007, New York City

565 Commercial Street, Provincetown, Massachusetts

Mailer once claimed that there wasn't a book he had written that he hadn't in some part worked on in Provincetown. The town suited his admiration for rugged masculinity—or at least it did in the 1960s. Bikers motored into town on Saturday nights and threw drunken parties on the beach. Fights broke out. Mailer liked getting drunk with fishermen and having arm-wrestling contests.

> ## "Words are, of course, the most powerful drug used by mankind."
>
> —Rudyard Kipling

In Rudyard Kipling's 1935 autobiography, *Something of Myself*, his very-last residence gets its very-own chapter, "The Very-Own House." As he wrote, upon visiting this house—"Bateman's"—for the first time, in 1892, "we reached her down an enlarged rabbit-hole of a lane. . . . We entered and felt her Spirit—her Feng Shui—to be good. We went through every room and found no shadow of ancient regrets, stifled miseries, nor any menace, though the 'new' end of her was three hundred years old."

Kipling soon snapped the property up, moving there with his wife, Carrie. It had been a wild decade for the Kiplings, beginning with their marriage in London in January 1892, in the "thick of an influenza epidemic, when the undertakers had run out of black horses and the dead had to be content with brown ones," as Kipling put it. Then, in 1894, came the wild success of *The Jungle Book*, inspired by the December 1892 birth of their first child, Josephine, who in 1899 would die of the tuberculosis that both she and Kipling contracted while away in America. After all of this, the Kiplings were ready to settle into this "good and peaceable place" in the High Weald hills of East Sussex.

The two-story sandstone gabled house, with its mullioned windows and diamond-shaped chimney stacks, sits within an estate that includes a mill once powered by the River Dudwell, which flows through the property. When the Kiplings purchased Bateman's, it was being used as a farmhouse, and had neither electricity nor running water.

Kipling believed the original owner of the house, built in 1634, was an ironmaster, which would have made sense, as iron ore had been mined in the area since the time of the Romans. He soon grew intrigued by the long history of the valley his study overlooked. Despite this interest, he could be unkind. As he wrote in his autobiography, "Of the little one-street village up the hill we only knew that, according to the guide-books, they came of a smuggling, sheep-stealing stock, brought more or less into civilization within the past three generations."

While resident in Bateman's, Kipling wrote "If—," his best-known poem, and a collection of fantasy stories, *Puck of Pook's Hill* (1906), named after a mound visible to the southwest. The study where he wrote was very much in the Edwardian style, featuring multiple globes, and in the days of use it would have been thick with the pungent aroma of his forty cigarettes a day.

Kipling's literary star has fallen so far that it can be easy to forget just how celebrated he was in his time. He was one of the best-known writers in the world when he moved into Bateman's, and in 1907 he would become the first English-language writer to be awarded the Nobel Prize in Literature. But his reputational decline came roughly in parallel with that of the British Empire, with which he was intrinsically linked.

Why Writers Use Pseudonyms

There is a long history of writers hiding behind aliases, involving acts of renewal,
a desire to keep the writer as private individual from the object of public
scrutiny, or as a way of circumventing the straitjacket of gender politics.
For example, in the past, women were not expected to be "serious" writers,
so were forced to adopt pseudonyms so as to get published. Novelist Mary Ann
Evans—one of the leading novelists, writers, and poets of the Victorian era—
used the pen name George Eliot.

What's in a name? Sometimes writers choose a name as an act of rebranding—or rebirth. Æ (George Russell) derived his pen name from the word "Æon," meaning "mystical being," which he thought would suit his poetic Celtic Revival needs. Saki (Hector Hugh Munro) took his name either from a character in the poem "Rubáiyát of Omar Khayyám" or from a South American monkey, to give himself a bit of distance from his dark short stories, which pilloried the high society within which he moved.

The French had a good run of single-named pseudonymous authors: Molière (Jean-Baptiste Poquelin), a stage name, perhaps taken from a town his company traveled through; Voltaire (François-Marie Arouet), to avoid imprisonment in the Bastille; Stendhal (Marie-Henri Beyle), who used more than a hundred pen names, mostly out of amusement.

Flann O'Brien (Brian O'Nolan) wrote under whichever name suited his mode of the moment, but generally used Flann for his fiction and Myles na gCopaleen for his newspaper work. Mark Twain (Samuel Clemens) took his name from his time working on the Mississippi River, "mark twain" being what riverboat captains would call out as a request for the river's depth to be measured.

Authors also often take up a pseudonym in an attempt to separate their public writer self from their private nonwriter self. John le Carré (David John Moore Cornwell) used a pen name because those who worked for the British Foreign Service at the time weren't allowed to publish books under their own names. He had seen the name on a London shopfront and thought a foreign-sounding name might stick in readers' heads better. Lewis Carroll (Charles Lutwidge Dodgson) came from a high-church family who might not have been keen to be associated with Carroll's rather surreal work. The name was chosen by his publishers from a list of possible names he had provided them. George Orwell (Eric Arthur Blair), who named himself after a river in southern England, wanted to avoid embarrassing his family with his memoir *Down and Out in Paris and London*. P. L. Travers (Helen Goff), who wrote the Mary Poppins series of books, preferred privacy to fame, and scoffed at the act of biography in general. And people have practically written PhDs theorizing on the identity of the Italian (?) author Elena Ferrante (?).

Other female authors have often found themselves persuaded to use a pseudonym in order to disguise their gender. George Eliot (Mary Ann Evans) wanted to ensure that her work would be treated with the same seriousness as that of her male counterparts. George

▲ Nineteenth-century French writer Marie-Henri Beyle used more than a hundred pseudonyms—Stendhal is the most frequently used, and best known. *Le Rouge et le Noir* (*The Red and the Black*) was his most celebrated novel.

▲ Mary Ann Evans, a.k.a. George Eliot. In her (anonymous) essay "Silly Novels by Lady Novelists," published in the *Westminster Review* in 1856, Eliot criticized most popular novels of the time written by and for women, objecting to their "silliness" and disregard for reality. Eliot wanted to be taken seriously as a novelist—at this time, using the name of a male author helped her achieve this.

Sand (Amandine Lucie Aurore Dupin), who used a pen name for a similar reason, also scandalized the mid-nineteenth-century French public by wearing men's clothing and smoking in public.

This practice continued well into the twentieth century. S. E. Hinton (Susan Eloise Hinton)—whose novel *The Outsiders*, written when she was sixteen, essentially launched the YA genre—was convinced by her publishers to conceal her gender by using her initials rather than her full name when the book was published in 1967. J. K. (Joanne—she has no middle name) Rowling's publishers thought boys wouldn't buy her books if they knew they were written by a woman.

Rowling also later wrote as Robert Galbraith to hide her fame, of which there is a long tradition: see Boz (Charles Dickens); Benjamin Black (John Banville); Stephen King (Richard Bachman); and Robert Markham (Kingsley Amis). There have been instances of male authors publishing under female names, as well as multiple authors (usually a married couple or siblings, and often in the crime genre) who write under a single name.

Jack London

Born: January 12, 1876, San Francisco, California
Died: November 22, 1916, Glen Ellen, California

The Cottage at the Beauty Ranch, Glen Ellen, Sonoma County, California

The wood-framed Cottage, originally built in the 1860s, was greatly
expanded to make it more liveable after Wolf House burned to the
ground. It had four guest rooms and "his and hers" sleeping porches.
The Beauty Ranch was later gifted to the state of California, and 800
out of its original 1,400 acres were preserved as Jack London State
Historic Park.

> "Life is not always a matter of holding good cards, but sometimes, playing a poor hand well."
>
> —Jack London

In 1897, having tired of laboring for meager pay in various jobs, including as an oyster pirate and a seal hunter, Jack London sought his fortune in the Klondike Gold Rush in Canada's Yukon Territory. A fortune he obtained, though it came through the stories the trip inspired rather than gold nuggets. His novel *The Call of the Wild* (1903) was an instant success, as were *The Sea Wolf* (1904) and *White Fang* (1906).

Not long before *White Fang* was published, London paid a visit to the editor of a literary magazine that ran many of his stories, and during this visit he fell in love with both a place (Glen Ellen, in Sonoma County, California) and a person (Charmian, the niece of his editor's wife). Charmian and London were a perfect match, both temperamentally and professionally, and in 1905, the year they were married, they purchased a plot of land in the Valley of the Moon (which was also the title of a 1913 novel by London). They named this land the Beauty Ranch (or, occasionally, the Ranch of Good Intentions).

The Beauty Ranch was paradise to London. As he wrote, "Between my legs is a beautiful horse. The air is wine. . . . Across Sonoma Mountain wisps of sea fog are stealing. . . . I have everything to make me glad I am alive." Visitors to the ranch (among them Sinclair Lewis and Ambrose Bierce) were frequent enough that London printed an information sheet to prepare them: "Our life here is something as follows: We rise early, and work in the forenoon. . . . You will find this a good place to work, if you have work to do. Or, if you prefer to play, there are horses, saddles, and rigs. In the summer we have a swimming pool."

But for London the ranch was more than just a writer's retreat; he wanted it to be a successful working farm, and he researched ancient agricultural practices to find the best way to make it happen. From 1911, London lived and wrote in the Cottage while waiting for completion of his "dream house": a fifteen-thousand-square-foot, twenty-six-room mansion called Wolf House, which was to be made from redwood logs and volcanic rock, with nine fireplaces. But just as Wolf House neared completion three years later, it was gutted by fire, a great financial loss that exacerbated the farm's already dire economic straits.

After the fire, London expanded the Cottage to a less modest three thousand square feet, including an annex that housed his study, where he wrote, with Charmian serving as both editor and typist. London gave himself the goal of writing a thousand words a day, and in his five years at the Cottage he wrote several novels as well as his memoir of drinking, *John Barleycorn*. Having long suffered from several ailments stemming both from his travels and from poor habits (including the use of morphine), London died in his sleeping porch at the Cottage at the age of just forty.

THE SOLACE OF NATURE

Beatrix Potter

Born: July 28, 1866, London
Died: December 22, 1943, Near Sawrey, UK

Hill Top Farm, Near Sawrey, Cumbria, UK

In her first decade writing as a children's author, Beatrix Potter
produced titles at a rate of about two a year, most of which she
created at Hill Top. The house, the garden, the nearby village—
as well, of course, as the animals—all served as constant
inspiration, which she repaid many times over with her
successful conservation efforts.

"There is a pleasure in the pathless woods,
There is a rapture on the lonely shore,
There is society, where none intrudes,
By the deep sea, and music in its roar:
I love not man the less, but Nature more."

—Lord Byron

"I would feel more optimistic about a bright
future for man if he spent less time proving
that he can outwit Nature and more time tasting
her sweetness and respecting her seniority."

—E. B. White

"There are some strange summer mornings in the
country, when he who is but a sojourner from
the city shall early walk forth into the fields,
and be wonder-smitten with the trance-like
aspect of the green and golden world."

—Herman Melville

Salman Rushdie

Born: June 19, 1947, Mumbai, India

Middle Pitts? Powys, Wales

The British government footed the bill for Rushdie's security detail (two officers, two drivers, and two armored cars, at a cost of £1 million a year), but it was up to Rushdie to pay for (and find) his accommodation, which the police would then vet and approve. He was very often at the mercy of friends—and former friends, such as Deborah Rogers, his former literary agent.

> **"What one writer can make in the solitude of one room is something no power can easily destroy."**
> —Salman Rushdie

Few twentieth-century writers' retreats could compare in drama to that necessitated by Salman Rushdie's 1988 novel *The Satanic Verses*. Inspired in part by the life of the prophet Muhammad, the novel triggered the issuing of a fatwa by Iran's Ayatollah Khomeini on Valentine's Day of the following year, calling for the author's death. Having learned of the fatwa after being called by a reporter at his home in London, Rushdie hung up and got in a car that was waiting to take him to do an interview. He would not return to the house.

After his interview, he went to the office of his literary agent in Chelsea—the Wylie Agency—and then to the funeral service of a friend, the author Bruce Chatwin. Martin Amis told Rushdie he was worried for him. Paul Theroux joked that they would be mourning Rushdie next. After the service, Rushdie vanished.

Now in hiding, Rushdie phoned his first wife, Clarissa, so he could speak to their son. Clarissa was a literary agent with the A. P. Watt agency. She said the agency's senior partner had a cottage in Oxfordshire that Rushdie could stay in for a few days. He did, and it was greatly appreciated, but not perfect—too exposed. He didn't know where to go next. Then he checked his voicemail. There was a message from Deborah Rogers— the literary agent Rushdie had thrown aside when he joined the Wylie Agency. She said she thought she could help. She had a farmhouse in Wales. It was called (perhaps) Middle Pitts. He could have it.

It was a good ruse. Anyone who knew Rushdie knew—or thought they knew—that he and Rogers had fallen out. No one would ever think to track him down through her. The place was perfect: a remote farmhouse in the hills of what is known as the "Welsh border country," as it abuts England. He met Rogers there the next day.

Life on the run turns mundane events into crises. A farmer who looked after Rogers's sheep saw that she was home and headed down to have a word with her. Rushdie had to duck underneath the kitchen counter. He couldn't blow his cover, no matter to whom; the risk was too great. Rushdie felt humiliated. Eventually the farmer left, and the reality of Rushdie's situation clanged home to him. Rogers said he could stay as long as he liked. But Rushdie knew he couldn't stay there long, only a matter of days, maybe weeks. This would be one among countless safe houses to come. He didn't write anything in this house.

Rushdie detailed his harrowing, decade-long life on the run in his 2012 book *Joseph Anton: A Memoir* (the title refers to the pseudonym he used, combining Joseph Conrad and Anton Chekhov). Although he calls the farmhouse in question "Middle Pitts" in the book, no record of this property could be found, leading one to believe that he may have changed the name of the house in order to protect the innocent—just to be safe.

William Wordsworth

Born: April 7, 1770, Cockermouth, UK
Died: April 23, 1850, Rydal, UK

Coleorton Hall, Coleorton, UK

The Winter Garden Wordsworth designed for
George Beaumont at Coleorton Hall
reflected, as he wrote in *The Prelude*, "The
passions that build up our human soul; / Not
with the mean and vulgar works of Man; /
But with high objects, with enduring things, /
With life and nature; purifying thus / The
elements of feeling and of thought."

> **"Wordsworth went to the lakes, but he was never a lake poet. He found in stones the sermons he had already hidden there."**
> —Oscar Wilde

Some retreats are given rather than chosen. And a person benefiting from the generosity of a patron could not have asked for better than Wordsworth found in Sir George Beaumont. "I esteem your friendship one of the best gifts of my life," Wordsworth wrote to Beaumont. "I and my family owe much to you and Lady Beaumont. . . . I speak of soul indebted to soul."

Apart from being a patron, Beaumont was also a close friend to Wordsworth, having bonded over a shared love of the Lake District landscape, which fits nicely with the link between friendship and landscape in Wordsworth's poetry. Beaumont had built Coleorton Hall in 1804 on land his family had owned since the fifteenth century, and he soon used it to the benefit of Britain's finest artists. Walter Scott started *Ivanhoe* there; John Constable sketched there. But Beaumont was particularly well inclined toward poets—and to Wordsworth in particular.

In 1806, the Beaumonts invited Wordsworth and his family to stay at Hall Farm, near Coleorton Hall, to write, but more specifically to design the Winter Garden. Wordsworth eagerly accepted the invitation, for just as he wrote of landscapes, he also wrote *in* landscapes. He wrote to Beaumont about his plans for the garden, wishing it to reflect their beloved Lake District: "For its own beauty, and for the sake of the hills and crags of the North, let [hollies] be scattered here in profusion." He looked to create a meditative space lined with evergreens and a border of majestic firs, and featuring a shell grotto designed by his sister Dorothy. He later wrote poems inspired by the garden.

Wordsworth's friendship with Beaumont was to age better than had his friendship with fellow poet Samuel Taylor Coleridge. In 1798, the two had copublished *Lyrical Ballads*, a collection that launched them to fame and included two of their best-known poems, "The Rime of the Ancient Mariner" and "Tintern Abbey." But from this literary pinnacle came a precipitous descent, brought about in large part due to Coleridge's attraction to Wordsworth's sister-in-law, Sara, who was staying with them at Coleorton.

Beaumont had invited Coleridge to stay at the house, and he joined them on Christmas Eve of that year. Coleridge had by this time separated from his wife, and was worse the wear from alcohol and opium use. Not long after Christmas, Wordsworth read aloud on successive evenings his "Poem to Coleridge," which he had been working on for eight years. But if Wordsworth hoped that the poem would raise Coleridge's spirits, he was to be disappointed. Coleridge in response wrote "To William Wordsworth, Composed on the Night After His Recitation of a Poem on the Growth of an Individual Mind," which made clear his growing disaffection with the group at Coleorton. Nor did Wordsworth's efforts help him fully realize his own poem, which he worked on for the rest of his life, though it was never finished, being published posthumously as *The Prelude*, considered nonetheless to be his magnum opus.

Breaking Away

William Burroughs

Born: February 5, 1914, St. Louis, Missouri
Died: August 2, 1997, Lawrence, Kansas

No. 9, Hotel El Muniria, Tangier, Morocco

Burroughs lived for four years in Room 9 at the Hotel El Muniria, which had access to a small walled garden, though Burroughs made little use of it; he tended to keep the shutters tightly closed. He came to be known by the locals as "el hombre invisible," a specter in trench coat and fedora floating past in an opiate miasma.

"Communication must become total and conscious before we can stop it."

—William Burroughs

By the time William Burroughs moved to Tangier in 1954, he had played on oil-slicked riversides in St. Louis, cut off the tip of his pinky finger in New York, studied medicine in Vienna, worked as an exterminator in Chicago, received a degree in English at Harvard, and shot his wife dead in Mexico City—though not necessarily in that order, as befits the time-defying Burroughs.

Burroughs was the definition of liminal, that favorite term of literary theorists, being simultaneously patrician and degraded, a precise mess, an elevated disgrace. This mix made Tangier in the 1950s a good match for the Beat writer, as it was a place of flux—part Europe, part Africa, part no place at all. The city was then known as the International Zone (or "Interzone," as Burroughs dubbed it), a neutral, demilitarized territory set up in 1924, run by a consortium of European nations. Known for its diversity and tolerance (particularly rare at that time), it became a hotbed of bohemianism—particularly for gay men. Burroughs had learned of the city through the work of the author Paul Bowles, who had lived in Tangier since World War II ended, and described it as a kind of paradise.

It was also cheap, and Burroughs was still in receipt of the monthly stipend paid to him by his parents (two hundred dollars a month), which meant he could devote himself either to majoun (a powerful cannabis concoction resembling fudge) or to writing—or, better yet, to both simultaneously, while also availing of the city's sexual permissiveness. After a short stint living on the Calle del los Arcos, above a male brothel, he moved into Room 9 at the Hotel El Muniria. Bowles, who visited Burroughs's small room, described it as strewn with loose papers and rat droppings, and in the introduction to *Naked Lunch* (1959), Burroughs claimed he had gone a year there without showering or changing his clothes, just shooting up. After overcoming his heroin-induced inertia, he tried writing conventional travel articles about the city, which he hoped his friend Allen Ginsberg might help get published, before turning his attention in earnest to fiction.

But, rarely for an author, Burroughs needed collaborators in order to bring a semblance of order to his scattered snippets of random passages, which (as always) had been written under the influence of a panoply of drugs. He sent missives to Ginsberg and Jack Kerouac, urging them to come to Tangiers and assist in piecing it together. Kerouac caved first, arriving in February 1957. Apart from working on Burroughs's book, they walked the beach, ate shrimp soup in medinas, gabbed at the Café de Paris. Burroughs brought binoculars onto the roof of Kerouac's apartment, they watched ships coming into port, and Kerouac got sick on Burroughs's arsenic-laced homemade opium. Ginsberg arrived with others and picked up where Kerouac left off, working in six-hour shifts and doing the lion's share of the editorial work. By June, they had two hundred pages of what would become *Naked Lunch*, the last literary work to face an obscenity trial in the United States.

"How often have I lain beneath rain on a strange roof, thinking of home."

—William Faulkner

"He who keeps fleeing, flees from his own past."

—Sumerian proverb

"There's nothing more difficult than saying goodbye to a house where you've suffered."

—Vasily Grossman

"I am going into the woods for another two or three years. I am going to try to do the best, the most important piece of work I have ever done. I am going to have to do it alone. I am going to lose what little bit of reputation I may have gained, to have to hear and know and endure in silence again all of the doubt, the disparagement and ridicule, the post-mortems that they are so eager to read over you even before you are dead."

—Thomas Wolfe replying to Scott Fitzgerald

Henry James

Born: April 15, 1843, New York City
Died: February 28, 1916, London

Garden Room, Lamb House, Rye, UK

James was immediately smitten with Lamb House, which had been built by a wine merchant in 1722 and was Rye's finest mansion. He did most of his writing in the Garden Room, which was situated perpendicular to the main house, and which he once referred to (perhaps facetiously) as "the temple of the muse." While the house can be visited, the room was destroyed by a bomb during World War II.

"In art economy is always beauty."

—Henry James

It is quite fitting that Henry James first encountered his final, beloved home through a piece of art. Having tired of his hectic London life, James propitiously happened upon a watercolor made by an architect friend, Edward Warren, in 1895. He was transfixed by the sketch, which showed the Garden Room of the eighteenth-century Lamb House in Rye, a village near the English Channel, fifty miles southeast of London. Visiting the house the following summer, he fell in love with it, and when, two years later, the opportunity arose, he snapped the property up, taking out a twenty-one-year lease and moving in following refurbishments, in June 1898.

James described Lamb House in a letter to his friend A. C. Benson: "It's such a place as I may, when pressed by the pinch of need, retire to with a certain shrunken decency and wither away in—in a fairly cleanly and pleasantly melancholy manner—towards the tomb. It is really good enough to be a kind of little, becoming, high door'd, brass knockered façade to one's life." Lamb House would quickly find its way into James's work, as the protagonist's home in *The Awkward Age* (1899), "suggestive of panelled rooms, of precious mahogany, of portraits of women dead, of coloured china glimmering through glass doors and delicate silver reflected on bared tables, the thing was one of those impressions of a particular period that it takes two centuries to produce."

The Garden Room that had initially drawn James to Lamb House was also where he wrote his final major novels, *The Wings of the Dove* (1902), *The Ambassadors* (1903), and *The Golden Bowl* (1904), and it was during this time that he began to be known as "The Master." During the colder months, he wrote in the Green Room, with its "coloured china glimmering through glass doors and delicate silver reflected on bared tables."

James quickly fell into a comfortable routine at Lamb House. He rose at eight and had breakfast in his bedroom (known as the King's Room, as King George I had slept there one night in 1726), then worked until ten, dictating to his secretary, Theodora Bosanquet. After lunch he walked with his dachshund, Maximilian, and in the evenings he revised that morning's writing. In *Henry James at Work* (published by Virginia and Leonard Woolf's Hogarth Press), Bosanquet reflected on James's precision, saying, "He took pains to pronounce every pronounceable letter, he always spelt out words which the ear might confuse with others, and he never left a single punctuation mark unuttered."

As James wrote to his sister, Alice, Lamb House was "the very calmest and yet cheerfullest that I could have dreamed—in the little old, cobble-stoned, grass-grown, red-roofed town, on the summit of its mildly pyramidal hill and close to its noble old church—the chimes of which will sound sweetly in my goodly old red-walled garden." And above it all was the Garden Room, "perched alongside of it on its high brick garden-wall—into which all these pleasant features together so happily 'compose'."

Writing in Prison

Whether behind bars for sociopolitical reasons, or persecuted for religious beliefs—or even occasionally for their gruesome crimes— through history captivity has often counterintuitively liberated the creative spirit, albeit in trying circumstances.

Several claimants to the world's first novels were written in prison. One was *Le Morte d'Arthur*, by Thomas Malory, who was quite familiar with incarceration, having been tried for murder, rape, robbery, and extortion, only to escape (twice) or be bailed out (twice). Malory worked on the Arthurian legends in 1469, while awaiting trial on charges that he had orchestrated a series of violent crimes. *Don Quixote*, published in 1605, is another candidate for the world's first novel. After escaping from slavery in Algiers, Miguel de Cervantes was working as a purchasing agent for the Spanish Armada, and any time authorities detected irregularities in his financial accounts, he was sent to jail. It was during one of these stints that he came up with the idea of writing a book using everyday language, leading him to write the novel that would bring him eternal fame.

Political persecution has been another avenue for authorial incarceration. Niccolò Machiavelli was a diplomat in Florence when the Medici family regained power in 1512. They viewed him as an enemy of the state and accused him of conspiracy, leading to him being arrested, tortured (having his hands bound behind his back and then being hung by them), imprisoned, and, following his release, banished from Florence. While in exile, he wrote *The Prince*, his treatise on power and politics. Fyodor Dostoevsky was sentenced in 1849 to four years of imprisonment in a

▲ Oscar Wilde in 1882, the year in which he made the first of two visits to the United States and Canada. The first-ever production of an Oscar Wilde play was in New York City in 1833, years before his success in London; *Vera; or, The Nihilists* was withdrawn after only one week.

labor camp in Siberia, for the crime of reading banned literature. There he witnessed acts of horrifying brutality and cruelty from guards and prisoners alike, but also encountered people of great decency. From these experiences he wrote *The House of the Dead*, a semi-autobiographical novel. Alexander Solzhenitsyn would have a depressingly similar trajectory a century later, writing his 1953 novel *One Day in the Life of Ivan Denisovich* from notes gathered while at a Siberian work camp.

Other authors were imprisoned for religious or social reasons. When John Bunyan was sentenced to twelve years in prison for his religious beliefs following the restoration of the English monarchy in 1660, he used his time to develop and write *The Pilgrim's Progress*, perhaps the most influential work of religious fiction ever written. Oscar Wilde was sentenced to two years of hard labor in Reading Gaol in 1895, for committing acts of homosexuality. While there, he wrote "De Profundis," a letter to his former lover, which would be published posthumously, and after being released, he wrote his final work, "The Ballad of Reading Gaol."

But, as Malory showed early on, some writers were imprisoned for fairly good reasons. The Marquis de Sade's crimes could fill several books. In 1785, while imprisoned in the Bastille prison, he wrote *The 120 Days of Sodom* in tiny script on a single, forty-foot-long scroll made of many smaller pieces of paper glued

▲ An engraving depicting the storming of the Bastille during the French Revolution, July 14, 1789. De Sade's scroll was found when the Bastille was stormed.

together. When the Bastille was stormed, marking the beginning of the French Revolution, de Sade was devastated, fearing that the scroll, which de Sade kept hidden within his cell wall, was lost forever.

William Sydney Porter, a bank teller, was charged with embezzlement in 1896, after which he fled to Honduras and started writing short stories. When he returned to America a year later he was sent to prison, where he continued writing short stories, later taking the name O. Henry, chosen in part to conceal his past as a felon. And finally, Jean Genet was in and out of prison for petty crimes for two decades, and he described his prison experiences in his first novel, *Our Lady of the Flowers* (1944), written while serving a sentence for burglary. The first version was confiscated by a prison guard and burned as contraband, but Genet just wrote it again.

Ernest Hemingway

Born: July 21, 1899, Oak Park, Illinois
Died: July 2, 1961, Ketchum, Idaho

Tift House, Key West, Florida

The Hemingways lived here with their two sons from 1931 to 1939, and Hemingway wrote in a studio above a former carriage house. It was his habit to write while standing, on a typewriter placed chest-high. In 1940, Hemingway left Pauline to live with his future third wife, Martha Gellhorn, in Cuba, but Pauline continued to live in the house with their sons until her death in 1951.

—Ernest Hemingway

It was the end of 1927, and Ernest Hemingway's second wife, Pauline, who was pregnant, wanted to leave Paris and return to America to have their baby. Hemingway's friend, the author John Dos Passos, suggested they try Key West, the outermost inhabited island in the Florida Keys archipelago. They arrived on the island and spent three years in rented housing, before Pauline found a house for sale at a tax auction in 1931, and her uncle bought it for them, for eight thousand dollars, as a wedding gift. This was 907 Whitehead Street, near the southern coast of the island (and the southernmost point of the contiguous United States).

This French Colonial-style house was built in 1851 by Asa Tift, a marine salvage wrecker, out of limestone quarried from the site by hand (likely by slaves owned by Tift). Unusually for Key West, the property's basement was consistently dry, underscoring the integrity of the original build (structurally if not morally). The house was derelict and in disrepair when the Hemingways moved in, and they spent the first few years restoring it, eventually hanging its walls with trophies from African safaris and hunting expeditions out West. There was scarce greenery on the grounds, as Key West wasn't then connected to water lines—rainwater being collected in a cistern on the roof—but Hemingway installed a boxing ring so he could spar with local pugilists. The ring was moved off site in 1937, however, when they installed a pool, at the cost of twenty thousand dollars, an astronomical amount at the time. It was the only pool within a hundred miles.

Hemingway was constantly on the move during the 1930s, most notably when reporting on the Spanish Civil War, and during much of this decade he spent summers in Wyoming and winters in Key West. When in Florida, he wrote during the morning, keeping his afternoons free for activity, such as big game sport fishing, catching marlin and tuna. To facilitate this interest, he bought a thirty-eight-foot customized wooden boat he named *Pilar*, which was also his nickname for Pauline (and would later become the name of a character fighting in the Spanish Civil War in his 1940 book *For Whom the Bell Tolls*). After the 1935 Labor Day hurricane, he used *Pilar* to ferry supplies to survivors.

Hemingway's writing studio was on the second floor of a former carriage house, which was connected to the master bedroom of the main house via a walkway; this meant that upon rising he could walk across and immediately begin work at his Woodstock typewriter. The studio windows overlooked the grounds, which were stalked by his polydactyl cats and pet peacocks. In the distance was Key West Lighthouse; Hemingway liked to joke that it guided him home when he was drunk of an evening.

Here he wrote his book on bullfighting, *Death in the Afternoon* (1932); an account of a safari he had taken, *Green Hills of Africa* (1935); and the short story collection *Winner Take Nothing* (1933). The work that drew most directly from his Florida home was his novel *To Have and Have Not* (1937), set in Depression-era Key West.

Zora Neale Hurston

Born: January 7, 1891, Notasulga, Alabama
Died: January 28, 1960, Fort Pierce, Florida

The Gingerbread District, Port-au-Prince, Haiti

A house in Pacot, the suburb of Port-au-Prince, was where Hurston spent seven weeks writing *Their Eyes Were Watching God* in a lovesick fury. She finished on December 19, 1936, and mailed the manuscript to her publisher, before setting off with the ethnomusicologist Alan Lomax, whom she had convinced to come from America to record the music of the people of Haiti.

> ## "People are trapped in history and history is trapped in them."
>
> —James Baldwin

Although James Baldwin, who had been raised in Harlem, had lived primarily in France from the age of twenty-four, he was in California in April 1968, when Martin Luther King Jr. was assassinated. Baldwin had known King, and had worked tirelessly in their shared fight for equal rights for all Americans, and he later attributed repressed grief from King's death to a series of mental breakdowns, leading to a stay at the American Hospital in Paris in October 1970.

A concerned friend persuaded Baldwin to visit Saint-Paul-de-Vence, in the French region of Provence, and Baldwin was so taken by the village that he soon moved into the Hameau Hotel, near the medieval ramparts. Located between the Alps and the French Riviera (also known as the Côte d'Azur, the narrow strip of coast that stretches roughly from Saint-Tropez to the Italian border), Saint-Paul-de-Vence is one of the region's many villages perched on hillsides, fragrant with flowering laurel trees, umbrella pines, thyme shrubs, and olive groves. When Baldwin moved there, it was a rather remote and sleepy town.

In March 1971, Baldwin inquired about the "For Rent" sign on a property across the street from the Hameau. He went to investigate. A green gate on the route de la Colle opened onto a long, cobblestone path that wound its way to a sprawling seventeenth-century stone farmhouse and gatehouse on ten acres overlooking the Mediterranean. From there, a passageway led to a back garden, where there was an apartment that had once been the painter Georges Braque's studio. Baldwin rented this apartment for a year, eventually taking over the entire property, paying for it in installments.

The age of the buildings meant that something always needed repairing, which Baldwin saw as a positive, in that "exasperating rigor is good for the soul," as it provided a purpose for the day, and he had "reached the age at which silence becomes a tremendous gift." He furnished the living room on the second floor with rustic Provençal furniture, in keeping with his preference for simple surroundings.

Immediately outside the kitchen doors, on the upper terrace of the house's garden, was a large table under a straw canopy on a platform surrounded by wildflowers, olive trees, orange trees, and laurels. This was dubbed the "Welcome Table," around which his many visitors would eat, drink, and discuss literature and the thorny political issues of the time, at dinners often stretching late into the night, accompanied by the noisy song of cicadas. During the day, rustic lunches—with plenty of local red wine and fresh bread—were prepared by a local woman named Valerie Sordello, who worked at the house for nearly all of Baldwin's years there and came to be considered as close as family.

Baldwin had long considered himself to be somewhat homeless, but he found a home within the community he formed among the people of Saint-Paul-de-Vence, helped a great deal by the fact that he spoke impeccable French. Over the course of his seventeen years in the town, the locals adopted Baldwin as one of their own. He often could be found in the Colombe d'Or hotel, heading into the village around four o'clock nearly every afternoon to chat with Yvonne Roux, who ran the hotel. Their friendship developed to such an extent that Baldwin named the main character of one of his novels after her: Clementine "Tish" Rivers, in *If Beale Street Could Talk* (1974), Clementine being Roux's middle name.

Baldwin's house went by several names. It was listed in the official records office as the "ancienne maison Baldwin," but locals called it "la maison de Jimmy," or just "Chez Baldwin." And beyond being a home, Chez Baldwin was a place of gathering. One of the aspects of the house that Baldwin found most appealing was that it offered plenty of space for guests to stay. The painter Beauford Delaney, an early influence on Baldwin in his days in New York, and a very close friend, was a regular at the house. He frequently worked in the garden, and painted at least two portraits of Baldwin there. Baldwin's brother David was also often in residence.

Many of Baldwin's musician friends visited the house over the years, including Nina Simone, Harry Belafonte, and Ray Charles, for whom Baldwin wrote several songs. Miles Davis would stay for a day or two any time he played the Jazz à Juan festival in nearby Antibes. In 1973, Josephine Baker, who also lived in the French Riviera, came for dinner, and the two lamented the fact that they had both seen it necessary to expatriate themselves from America.

Although his better-known works were written before moving to Saint-Paul-de-Vence (including his first novel, *Go Tell It on the Mountain* (1953), which he only began writing after he first moved to France in 1948), he remained productive during his years there. His days were devoted to answering the copious mail he received from around the world, and he generally wrote at night, at his sturdy typewriter. A year after moving to Saint-Paul-de-Vence, Baldwin published a collection of nonfiction, *No Name in the Street* (1972), followed by *If Beale Street Could Talk* in 1974. Two years later came Baldwin's only children's book, *Little Man, Little Man* (1976), and in the same year he published a book on cinema and popular culture, *The Devil Finds Work*. Baldwin's sixth and final novel, *Just Above My Head*, followed in 1979, and four years later, he published his only collection of poems, *Jimmy's Blues*. His final two published works, the essay collection *The Price of the Ticket* and *The Evidence of Things Not Seen*, which documented a series of murders of children in Atlanta, both appeared in 1985.

At the time of his death, Baldwin was working on a play entitled *The Welcome Table*, named for the table at Chez Baldwin. His notes on the play show just how much influence his final home had on his work, and in particular the aspects that were celebrated around this table—multinationalism, multiculturalism, intellectual curiosity, freedom from racism or homophobia, and a desire to embrace joy in life to whatever extent possible.

James Joyce

Born: February 2, 1882, Dublin, Ireland
Died: January 13, 1941, Zurich, Switzerland

When the author, doctor, and bon vivant Oliver St. John Gogarty first met James Joyce, in a Dublin tram, he noted that the slight young man with "smoke-blue eyes" and a "slight golden beard, like a haze" carried under his arm a roll of vellum that contained, he later discovered, the twenty-two-year-old author's poems—part of what would later become the collection *Chamber Music*. This meeting marked the start of a brief, fiery literary adventure.

According to Gogarty (admittedly not always the most reliable of narrators), Joyce approached him in the spring of 1904 with the idea of renting a demilitarized Martello tower, a round fortress "built of cut granite and shaped like a sculptor's mallet," in Sandycove, a seaside village eight miles south of Dublin. Shortly afterward, they traveled to the tower for the first time. The entrance was reached by a ladder that led to a door

Sandycove Martello tower, Dublin, Ireland

Gogarty dreamed that the tower would serve as a center of culture from which he and Joyce could "hellenize" Ireland. But Joyce was skeptical from the start, and he ended up living there for only six days. Within a month, he and Nora Barnacle had left Ireland forever. Gogarty and Trench later became the models for the *Ulysses* characters Buck Mulligan and Haines, respectively.

"There is not past, no future; everything flows in an eternal present."

—James Joyce

halfway up the wall on the side opposite the sea. Joyce produced a ten-inch copper key and unlocked the metal door, which resisted when pushed, as it hadn't been opened in years. They then descended steps into a large circular room, flushing pigeons who fled outward through narrow windows designed to facilitate shooting by the fort's defenders. Another door revealed a stairwell, which they ascended, emerging onto a roof with chin-high walls over which could be found a 360-degree view of Dublin and its bay. "We could stand a siege here," Gogarty has Joyce remarking. To which Gogarty replied, "It's a good retreat for those who like retreating."

Although rental of the property had not yet been secured, Gogarty says Joyce "took possession" of the tower by laying his roll of poems on the shelf. The tower in hand, Gogarty set about finding furnishing for future residence, and spreading word around Dublin that he had rented the tower to "house the Bard" (i.e. Joyce), who was broke as usual, and needed "a year in which to finish his novel"—*Stephen Hero*, which Joyce would first abandon and later cannibalize to create *A Portrait of the Artist as a Young Man*, published in 1916.

Following the death of his mother in August 1903, Joyce had spent the year scratching together a scarce living in Dublin, reviewing books, teaching, and singing, and otherwise drinking and roaming the streets. On June 16, 1904, he went on the literary world's most famous first date, with his future wife, Nora Barnacle, a day that would later be memorialized in his novel *Ulysses*. At the end of that August, he was forced to leave the rooms he had been renting in town, and had been staying in a variety of houses for a few days. Meanwhile, Gogarty finally had taken up residence at the tower, and had invited his fellow student at Oxford, Samuel Chenevix Trench, to stay. Trench, an Englishman, was obsessed with all things Irish. Gogarty described him as a "zealot," who "removed the shades of our lamps and filled the tower with smoke until Irish glass should appear to take their places." Trench also worked as an assistant to George Russell (a.k.a. the poet Æ), the editor at *The Irish Homestead*, a weekly publication that ran, under the name Stephen Daedalus, Joyce's story "Eveline" (later to appear in *Dubliners*) the day after he moved into the tower.

Finally, on September 9, Joyce joined them at the tower. They feasted on lobsters bought from local fishermen. Procured milk, butter, bacon, and eggs. Dined on metal plates (which they burned clean in the fire rather than washing them) atop the roof, al fresco, with the gun emplacement serving as a table, the gun having been long since removed. Drank pints at Murray's tavern nearby, or in town at Davy Byrne's pub (which later featured in *Ulysses*). Left the front door open to chase away the gloom. Gogarty convinced Joyce to let him shave off his beard, to "offer up [his] whiskers to the Muses," using the "lovely soft water in the storage tank."

▶ Joyce's apartment within the Martello tower, as recreated by the museum that now inhabits it. Note the rather coy inclusion of the black panther that prowled through Trench's nightmare, thus ending Gogarty's dream of a Celtic literary revolution—and sowing the seed for Joyce's.

Joyce, who had a job teaching at a school in an adjacent village, was typically diffident during his residence here, refusing, for example, to swim at the Forty Foot bathing spot at the foot of the tower. Gogarty wrote, "Sometimes when I would be lolling on the roof, getting a tan and feeling the sun pulsating on my skin, I would think of Joyce in the dark room underneath and invite him to come out into the air"—to no avail. One visitor to the tower described Joyce as "a singer of songs which spring from the deepest currents of life . . . [who] listened in silence, and when we went on the roof he disposed himself restfully to drink in the glory of the morning."

While at the tower, Joyce wrote part if not all of "He Who Hath Glory Lost," a barbed little poem that one of his biographers claims was aimed at Gogarty. He wouldn't have time for much more writing, though. On the night of September 14, Trench, awaking in a panic from a nightmare involving a black panther, grabbed a revolver he had secreted away and fired a shot or two. Gogarty managed to relieve Trench of the gun, and calmed him down to the extent that he fell back asleep, only to awaken screaming again shortly after. This time it was Gogarty who fired the gun, bringing a shelf of pots and pans crashing down onto Joyce's head, after which, as Gogarty put it, he "rose solemnly, dressed himself in his faded trousers, pulled on his shirt and his white yachting cap and his tennis shoes, took his ashplant cane and left the tower and never came back."

It being the middle of the night, Joyce had to walk back to the city. Later he wrote to a friend, asking him to go to the tower and pack the few belongings he had abandoned—including the rolled-up manuscript of his verses, still on the shelf—so he could collect them the next day.

"Happiness is not only a hope,
but also in some strange
manner a memory . . .
we are all kings in exile."

—G. K. Chesterton

"Any writer, I suppose, feels
that the world into which he
was born is nothing less than
a conspiracy against the
cultivation of his talent . . ."

—James Baldwin

"... every writer becomes an exile simply by venturing into literature, and every reader becomes an exile simply by opening a book."

—Roberto Bolaño

"One can run away from anything but oneself."

—Stefan Zweig

Gore Vidal

Born: October 3, 1925, West Point, New York
Died: July 31, 2012, Los Angeles, California

Chateau Marmont, 8221 Sunset Boulevard, Los Angeles, California

The Marmont was said to house celebrities either on the way up or on the way down, and Vidal in the 1950s was most definitely still one of the former. It was also the go-to place to stay for East Coasters when they were in town. These factors, along with sun, sex, booze, and invisibility (when you wanted it), made the Marmont an ideal refuge.

"Gore is a man without an unconscious."

—Italo Calvino

In 1956, Gore Vidal signed a four-year contract with Metro-Goldwyn-Mayer as a scriptwriter. Where else would he stay while in town but on Sunset Boulevard, at the Chateau Marmont, Los Angeles's answer to the Chelsea Hotel?

The sixty-three-room Marmont was built (in faintly ridiculous fairy-tale-castle style, with gables and a big turret, in 1929) as an apartment house, which meant that every unit was self-enclosed, and there was no lobby, restaurant, or bar. As a result, the chateau couldn't give you luxury (it was pretty shabby in the 1950s), but it had a great location, and it offered privacy par excellence. Plus, all were welcome—black, white, straight, gay—as long as they paid their bill. Although his 1948 debut novel, *The City and the Pillar*, depicted gay romance without shame (unheard of at the time), Vidal didn't then speak openly about his sexuality; at the Marmont he could be himself.

Vidal also could experience the youthful frivolity he'd missed out on by serving in the army during World War II, spending much of his time at the Marmont drinking, carousing, networking—and lounging at the pool with Paul Newman, with whom he had worked on a teleplay about Billy the Kid. Vidal's mother would occasionally come to stay with him there, which likely curtailed the carousing. Vidal even threw himself a birthday party in his suite, which was reported on by a local gossip columnist, who of course didn't name any names. During Vidal's time working for MGM, he was brought in to rework the screenplay for *Ben-Hur* (1959)—inserting, he later claimed, a gay subtext between the two main characters. He also said they had to keep this fact from Charlton Heston so that he wouldn't refuse to shoot the scene. Hollywood had chewed up and spat out many a starry-eyed writer, but Vidal was far too savvy for that.

Directly across Sunset from the Marmont during Vidal's stay stood a billboard advertising the Sahara Hotel in Las Vegas, which consisted of a sky-blue backdrop for a coyly exhibitionistic and scantily (yet patriotically) clad cowgirl-majorette showgirl statue, mechanized so that she spun on a silver dollar like a record. Vidal had a good view of this polychrome icon from his room. He said that, to awake in the morning with a hangover and see the ceaselessly spinning, sombrero-wielding showgirl, was to know what death would be like. The statue recurs throughout his 1968 novel *Myra Breckinridge*, a satire on American culture that attempted to tear down preconceived notions around gender and sexuality. It was a far cry from the historical novels for which he was known. Much of the novel was set at the Marmont, and its lead character, a transgender woman hellbent on using Los Angeles as a launchpad for world domination, found the spinning showgirl to be beautiful and omnipotent, a sort of alter ego, and a mesmerizing symbolic distillation of Hollywood.

The showgirl was taken down in 1966 and replaced with a sixty-foot-tall Marlboro Man—precisely the kind of retrograde hypermasculine figure Myra would have enjoyed forcing into submission.

World Map of Writer Locations

1 Allen Ginsberg
2 Alice Munro
3 Anton Chekhov
4 Arthur C. Clarke
5 Arthur Conan Doyle
6 Beatrix Potter
7 Charles Dickens
8 Chimamanda Ngozi Adichie

9 Dashiell Hammett
10 Dylan Thomas
11 Edith Wharton
12 Emily Dickinson
13 Ernest Hemingway
14 Franz Kafka
15 George Bernard Shaw
16 George Orwell
17 Gore Vidal

18 Henry James
19 Henry Thoreau
20 Herman Melville
21 Honoré de Balzac
22 Jack Kerouac
23 Jack London
24 James Baldwin
25 James Joyce
26 J. D. Salinger

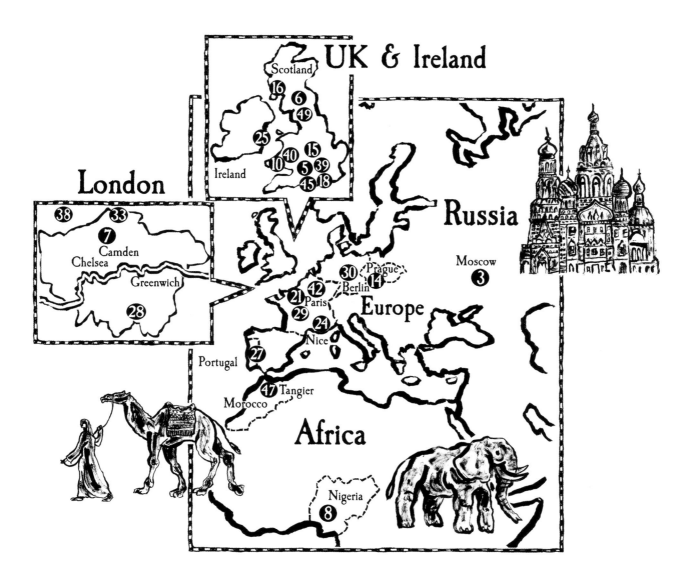

London
- 38
- 33
- 7 Camden
- Chelsea
- Greenwich
- 28

UK & Ireland
- Scotland
- 16
- 6
- 49
- 25
- Ireland
- 10 40 15
- 5 39
- 45 18

Russia
- Moscow
- 3

Europe
- 30 Prague
- 14 Berlin
- 21 42
- Paris
- 29
- 24
- Nice
- 27
- Portugal
- 47 Tangier
- Morocco

Africa
- Nigeria
- 8

27 J. K. Rowling	35 Nathaniel Hawthorne	43 Sylvia Plath
28 Judith Kerr	36 Norman Mailer	44 Toni Morrison
29 Marcel Proust	37 Ray Bradbury	45 Virginia Woolf
30 Margaret Atwood	38 Roald Dahl	46 Willa Cather
31 Marilynne Robinson	39 Rudyard Kipling	47 William Burroughs
32 Mark Twain	40 Salman Rushdie	48 William Faulkner
33 Martin Amis	41 F. Scott Fitzgerald	49 William Wordsworth
34 Maya Angelou	42 Simone de Beauvoir & Jean-Paul Sartre	50 Zora Neale Hurston

Bibliography

"1648 Rockland Avenue." Victoria Heritage Foundation. www. victoriaheritagefoundation.ca/HReg/Rockland/Rockland1648.html.

"A Henry James Centenary Exhibition." *Colby Quarterly*, volume 1, issue 3, June 1943.

Abbott, Kate. "Nathaniel Hawthorne and Herman Melville at Arrowhead." *Berkshire Eagle*, August 7, 2013.

Achebe, Chinua. *There Was a Country: A Personal History of Biafra*. New York: Penguin Press, 2012.

Adichie, Chimamanda Ngozi. "Strangely Personal: Growing Up in Chinua Achebe's House." Pen America. Accessed April 17, 2020. www.pen.org/strangely-personal-growing-up-in-chinua-achebes-house.

Amis, Martin. *Experience*. New York: Vintage Publishing, 2001.

Arthur Conan Doyle Encyclopedia website. www.arthur-conan-doyle.com.

Arthur Conan Doyle Relaxes with his Family at Windlesham (film). BFI website, 1929. www.player.bfi.org.uk/free/film/watch-arthur-conan-doyle-relaxes-with-his-family-at-windlesham-1929-online.

Athitakis, Mark. "Saluting *Myra Breckenridge* on its 50th anniversary." *Los Angeles Times*, February 23, 2018.

Atwood, Margaret. *Dire Cartographies: The Roads to Ustopia—The Handmaid's Tale and the MaddAddam Trilogy*. New York: Vintage Books, 2011.

Atwood, Margaret. "Margaret Atwood on What 'The Handmaid's Tale' Means in the Age of Trump." *New York Times*, March 10, 2017.

Bakewell, Sarah. *At the Existentialist Café: Freedom, Being, and Apricot Cocktails*. New York: Other Press, 2016.

Balaban, Judy. "The Gore They Loved." *Vanity Fair*, February 2013.

Ballinger, Lucy. "How Dylan Thomas's Writing Shed Inspired Roald Dahl." *BBC News* website, September 14, 2016. www.bbc.com/news/uk-wales-37342271.

Banville, John. "Novels were never the same after Henry James." *Irish Times*, October 7, 2017.

Barnes, Bart. "J. D. Salinger, 91; *Catcher in the Rye* author became famous recluse." *Washington Post*, January 29, 2010.

"Bateman's." National Trust website. www.nationaltrust.org.uk/batemans.

Beauvoir, Simone de. *Letters to Sartre*. Translated and edited by Quintin Hoare. Editions Gallimard, 1990.

Blotner, Joseph. *Faulkner: A Biography*. London: Chatto and Windus, 1974.

Bosanquet, Theodora. *Henry James at Work*. Ann Arbor: University of Michigan Press, 2007.

Boyd, Valerie. *Wrapped in Rainbows: The Life of Zora Neale Hurston*. New York: Scribner, 2003.

Bradbury, Ray. "Fahrenheit 451 Revisited." *UCLA Magazine*, Summer 2002.

Brockes, Emma. "A Life in Writing: Marilynne Robinson." *Guardian*, May 30, 2009.

Brockes, Emma. "Toni Morrison: 'I want to feel what I feel. Even if it's not happiness'." *Guardian*, April 13, 2012.

Brown, David S. *Paradise Lost: A Life of F. Scott Fitzgerald*. Cambridge: Harvard University Press, 2017.

Burroughs, William S. *Naked Lunch*. New York: Grove Press, 1959.

Bury, Liz. "Charles Dickens's Kent mansion to be opened to public as museum." *Guardian*, September 6, 2013.

Charles Dickens Letters Project website. www.dickensletters.com.

Charters, Ann and Samuel Charters. *Brother-Souls: John Clellon Holmes, Jack Kerouac, and the Beat Generation*. Jackson: University Press of Mississippi, 2010.

Chekhov, Anton. *Letters of Anton Chekhov to His Family and Friends*. Translated by Constance Garnett. New York: The Macmillan Company, 1920.

"Chez Baldwin." National Museum of African American History & Culture website. www.nmaahc.si.edu/explore/exhibitions/chez-baldwin.

Chilton, Martin. "Jack London: The reckless, alcoholic adventurer who wrote *The Call of the Wild*." *Independent*, February 20, 2020.

Chilton, Martin. "The odd life of *Catcher in the Rye* author J. D. Salinger." *The Independent*, January 1, 2019.

Cowan, Alison Leigh. "Salinger's Last Known Manhattan Home." *New York Times*, January 29, 2010.

Currey, Mason. *Daily Rituals: How Great Minds Make Time, Find Inspiration, and Get to Work*. New York: Picador, 2013.

Dahl, Roald. *Boy: Tales of Childhood*. New York: Cape, 1984.

Day-Lewis, Tamasin. "Am I the 'Leggy Temptress' in Martin Amis's New Novel?" *Telegraph*, February 17, 2010.

Dearborn, Mary. *Ernest Hemingway: A Biography*. New York: Penguin Random House, 2018.

Delbanco, Andrew. *Melville: His World and Work*. New York: Random House, 2006.

Dickinson, Emily. *Emily Dickinson: Selected Letters*. Edited by Thomas H. Johnson. Cambridge: Harvard University Press, 1971.

Donadio, Rachel. "Battling to Save James Baldwin's Home in the South of France." *New York Times*, April 4, 2017.

Dreifus, Clauda. "A Conversation with Arthur C. Clarke: An Author's Space Odyssey and His Stay at the Chelsea." *New York Times*, October 26, 1999.

Duncan, Allistair. *No Better Place: Arthur Conan Doyle, Windlesham and Communication with the Other Side*. London: MX Publishing, 2015.

Dylan Thomas Boathouse website. www.dylanthomasboathouse.com.

Ellmann, Richard. *James Joyce*. Oxford: Oxford University Press, 1999.

Fay, Sarah. "Marilynne Robinson, The Art of Fiction No. 198." *Paris Review*, Issue 186, Fall 2008.

Ferris, Paul. *Dylan Thomas: The Biography*. Tal-y-bont: Y Lolfa, 2006.

"Finding Henry James' Place at Lamb House." National Trust website. www.nationaltrust.org.uk/lamb-house/features/finding-henry-james-place-at-lamb-house.

Flamm, Matthew. "The New York Stroll: Walking Where Kerouac Did." *New York Times*, November 30, 1997.

Floyd, Janet and Inga Bryden. *Domestic Space: Reading the Nineteenth-Century Interior*. Manchester: Manchester University Press, 1999.

Forster, John. *The Life of Charles Dickens*. Cambridge University Press, 2011.

Freeman, John. "Off the Road: Kerouac's Forgotten Abode." *Guardian*, September 3, 2007.

Friedkin, William. "In the Footsteps of Marcel Proust." *New York Times*, May 15, 2017.

Fuss, Diana. "Interior Chambers: The Emily Dickinson Homestead," *Differences: A Journal of Feminist Cultural Studies*, 10.3, 1998.

Fuss, Diana. *The Sense of an Interior: Four Rooms and the Writers that Shaped Them*. Abingdon: Routledge, 2004.

"Golden Lane." Prague Castle website. www.hrad.cz/en/prague-castle-for-visitors/objects-for-visitors/golden-lane-10334.

Grace, Michael L. "J. D. Salinger (*Catcher in the Rye*) was a cruise director aboard Swedish America Line's MS *Kungsholm* in 1941 . . ." Cruise Line History website, September 4, 2013. www.cruiselinehistory.com/j-d-salinger-catcher-in-the-rye-was-a-cruise-director-aboard-swedish-america-lines-ms-kungsholm-in-1941.

Guest, Katy. "Judith Kerr: If Carlsberg Made Grannies . . ." *Independent*, October 22, 2011.

Guinness, Bunny. "Monk's House, the garden that inspired Virginia Woolf." *Telegraph*, October 15, 2013.

Habegger, Alfred. *My Wars Are Laid Away in Books: The Life of Emily Dickinson*. New York: Modern Library, 2001.

Harris, Oliver and Ian MacFadyen, eds. *Naked Lunch@50: Anniversary Essays*. Carbondale: Southern Illinois University Press, 2009.

Hemingway Home website. www.hemingwayhome.com.

Heully, Gustave. "Why Bullwinkle Moose Stands Statuesque on the Strip." WEHOville website, July 1, 2013. www.wehoville.com/2013/07/01/ever-wonder-why-bullwinkle-moose-stands-statuesque-on-the-strip.

Hoby, Hermione. "Toni Morrison: 'I'm writing for black people . . . I don't have to apologise.'" *Guardian*, April 25, 2015.

Holroyd, Michael. *Bernard Shaw, 1898–1918: The Pursuit of Power*. London: Chatto & Windus, 1989.

Hook, Andrew. *F. Scott Fitzgerald: A Literary Life*. London: Palgrave Macmillan, 2002.

Hurston, Zora Neale. *Dust Tracks on a Road*. New York: HarperCollins, 2010.

Jack London Society website. www.jacklondonsociety.org.

James Joyce Centre website. www.jamesjoyce.ie.

James Joyce Tower & Museum website. www.joycetower.ie.

James, Henry. *Hawthorne*. London: Macmillan and Co., 1879.

James, Henry. *The Correspondence of Henry James and the House of Macmillan, 1877–1914*. Edited by Rayburn S. Moore. New York: Springer, 1993.

Jennings, La Vinia Delois, ed. *Zora Neale Hurston, Haiti, and Their Eyes Were Watching God*. Evanston: Northwestern University Press, 2013.

Jordison, Sam. "Beat and Dust: Tangier's Tang of History." *Guardian*, November 23, 2010.

Kafka, Franz. *Letters to Friends, Family, and Editors*. Translated by Richard and Clara Winston. New York: Schocken Books, 1977.

Keating, Sara. "Judith Kerr: The Only Bedtime Story my Children Liked was about a Tiger." *Irish Times*, February 21, 2017.

Kellogg, Carolyn. "Ray Bradbury and the dime-at-a-time typewriter of *Fahrenheit 451*." *Los Angeles Times*, June 6, 2012.

Kerouac, Jack and Allen Ginsberg. *Jack Kerouac and Allen Ginsberg: The Letters*. Edited by Bill Morgan and David Stanford. New York: Viking, 2010.

Kipling, Rudyard. *Something of Myself*. London: Macmillan, 1937.

Kramer, Barbara. *Toni Morrison: A Biography of a Nobel Prize-Winning Writer*. Berkeley Heights: Enslow Publishers, 2013.

Labor, Earle. *Jack London: An American Life*. New York: Farrar, Straus and Giroux, 2014.

Larson, Susan. "William Faulkner House in New Orleans has a Story in Every Room." *Times-Picayune*, November 7, 2009.

Lear, Linda. *Beatrix Potter: A Life in Nature*. London: St Martin's Griffin, 2016.

Lee, Hermione. "Writers' rooms: Virginia Woolf." *Guardian*, June 13, 2008.

Leeming, David. *James Baldwin: A Biography*. New York: Arcade, 2015.

Lennon, J. Michael. "Norman Mailer's Provincetown." Norman Mailer Society website, April 28, 2015. www.normanmailer.us/norman-mailer-s-provincetown-66943d75e164.

Levitt, Aimee. "From Mark Twain to Jonathan Franzen, St. Louis has been home to a surprising number of great writers." *Riverfront Times*, August 18, 2010.

Levy, Shawn. *The Castle on Sunset: Life, Death, Love, Art, and Scandal at Hollywood's Chateau Marmont*. New York: Penguin Random House, 2020.

Lidz, Franz. "Britain's Lake District Was Immortalized by Beatrix Potter, But Is Its Future in Peril?" *Smithsonian Magazine*, May 2018.

London, Jack. *John Barleycorn*. New York: The Century Company, 1913.

Luria, Sarah. "The Architecture of Manners: Henry James, Edith Wharton, and the Mount." *American Quarterly*, volume 49, no. 2, June 1997, Johns Hopkins University Press.

Lycett, Andrew. *Conan Doyle: The Man Who Created Sherlock Holmes*. London: Weidenfeld & Nicolson, 2008.

Lycett, Andrew. *Dylan Thomas: A New Life*. London: Orion Publishing, 2004.

Lycett, Andrew. *Rudyard Kipling*. London: Hachette, 2015.

Mailer, Norman. *The Naked and the Dead*, Fiftieth Anniversary Edition. London: Picador, 2000.

Maison de Balzac website. www.maisondebalzac.paris.fr/en/decouvrir-le-musee/history-museum.

Mallick, Heather. "Alice Munro's house should be a museum." *Toronto Star*, October 19, 2013.

Mark Twain Project website. www.marktwainproject.org.

Masset, Claire. "Beatrix Potter's Hill Top." *National Trust Magazine*, summer 2016 issue.

McKinney, Cristóbal. "Marilynne Robinson, According to her Students and Friends: Former Students Recall Robinson's Influence on their Careers." Iowa Now website, September 9, 2016. www.now.uiowa.edu/2016/09/marilynne-robinson-according-her-students-and-friends.

Mikhail, E.H., ed. *James Joyce: Interviews and Recollections*. London: Palgrave Macmillan, 1990.

Miller, Edwin Haviland. *Salem Is My Dwelling Place: A Life of Nathaniel Hawthorne*. Iowa City: University of Iowa Press, 1991.

Minter, David. *William Faulker: His Life and Work*. Baltimore: John Hopkins UP, 1980.

Morgan, Bill. *I Celebrate Myself: The Somewhat Private Life of Allen Ginsberg*. New York: Penguin Books, 2007.

Morgan, Bill. *The Typewriter Is Holy: The Complete, Uncensored History of the Beat Generation*. New York: Free Press, 2010.

Morrison, Toni. *The Bluest Eye*. New York: Vintage International, 2007.

Morrison, Toni. *The Source of Self-Regard: Selected Essays, Speeches, and Meditations*. New York: Alfred A. Knopf, 2019.

Morrow, Adrian. "Honour Alice Munro by turning properties into tourist attractions, says publisher." *Globe and Mail*, October 16, 2013.

"Norman Mailer's USA." YouTube video, interview for *Fem Amerikanare*, c.1970s.

Painter, George D. *Marcel Proust: A Biography*. London: Pimlico, 1996.

Pegg, Matthew. *Wordsworth in Leicestershire*. Coalville: Mantle Lane Press, 2017.

Pierpont, Claudia Roth. "A Society of One: Zora Neale Hurston, American Contrarian." *New Yorker*, February 17, 1997 issue.

Pires, Candice. "On the Prowl: Inside the Home of the Author of *The Tiger Who Came to Tea*." *Guardian*, March 4, 2017.

Plath, Sylvia. *The Unabridged Journals of Sylvia Plath: 1950–1962*. Edited by Karen V. Kukil. New York: Anchor Books, 2000.

Plimpton, George. "Maya Angelou, The Art of Fiction No. 119." *Paris Review*, Issue 116, fall 1990.

Pocock, Emma. "J. K. Rowling Debunks *Harry Potter* Inspiration Claims." *Forbes*, May 24, 2020.

"President Obama & Marilynne Robinson: A Conversation in Iowa." *New York Review of Books*, November 5, 2015.

Rae, Jeanne. "Wordsworth in Leicestershire." Wordsworth Trust website, April 10, 2017. www.wordsworth.org.uk/blog/2017/04/10/wordsworth-in-leicestershire.

Raskin, Jonah. *American Scream: Allen Ginsberg's Howl and the Making of the Beat Generation*. Berkeley: University of California Press, 2006.

Rayfield, Donald. *Anton Chekhov: A Life*. Evanston: Northwestern University Press, 2000.

Robb, Graham. *Balzac: A Biography*. New York: W.W. Norton & Co., 1995.

Ross, Catherine Sheldrick. *Alice Munro: A Double Life*. Toronto: ECW Press, 1993.

Rozzo, Mark. "Secrets of the Chateau Marmont." *Vanity Fair*, February 4, 2019.

Rushdie, Salman. *Joseph Anton: A Memoir*. New York: Random House, 2012.

Picture Credits

Every effort has been made to trace the copyright holders of the photos in this book. In order for any errors or omissions to be corrected in future editions, please contact Elephant Book Company.

Front cover, interior illustrations, and map: Robert Littleford

akg-images: 159 /Album: 157 /I.D.E.A. S.p.A.: 139 /Olivier Martel: 40 /NTB scanpix/Inge Gjellesvik: 105 /© Omikron/SCIENCE SOURCE: 33 /picture-alliance/Fred Stein: 125 /Pictures From History: 122, 127 /TT News Agency: 81 /UIG: 51 /ullstein bild: 75 /ullstein bild/B. Friedrich: 61 /ullstein bild/ Teutopress: 111 /Michael Zapf: 85

Alamy: /Alain Le Garsmeur: 161 /Jeff Morgan 23, 43

Bibliothèque nationale de France (BnF), Paris, France © BnF, Dist. RMN-Grand Palais: 35

British Library: 63

Christie's: 41r

Fred De Witt/courtesy of the Orange County Regional History Center: 27

Elephant Book Company: 78

Estate of William S. Burroughs: 145

Getty: /Photo © Allen Ginsberg/CORBIS/Corbis via Getty Images: 77 /Photo by Rune Hellestad/Corbis via Getty Images: 43 /Photo by Kenneth Stevens/Fairfax Media via Getty Images: 29 /Photo by Bernard Gotfryd/Getty Images: 61 /Photo by Reg Innell/Toronto Star via Getty Images: 21 /Photo by Craig Herndon/Washington Post via Getty Images: 71

The Granger Collection, New York: 46

Photo courtesy of Heritage Auctions: 12

Copyright © Elisa Leonelli via Calisphere: 49

Courtesy of Elizabeth Pedinotti Haynes: 67

Library of Congress: 11, 17, 25, 37, 39, 46, 95, 101, 107, 129, 133, 149, 153, 155 /Fabian Bachrach: 55 /New York World–Telegram & Sun Collection: 155

New York Academy of Medicine Library: 99

Private collection: 118

Public domain via Wikimedia Commons: 41tl, 59, 86, 90, 97, 131tr, 135, 141, 150

Courtesy of Victoria Samburanis: 66

Smithsonian Institution/National Portrait Gallery, Washington, DC: 117

Shutterstock: /Rupert Krapfenbauer 65 /AC Manley 102 /SydsPics Photography 87 /German Vizulis 131tl, 151

TopFoto: /Photoshot/Guillem Lopez/Avalon: 15

Courtesy of the University of Iowa, Office of Strategic Communication; Photographer, Justin Torner: 103

Carl Van Vechten photograph collection/Library of Congress: 69, 88, 165

Winokur-Munblit Collection of the Russian Empire Postcards/Library of Congress: 115

Acknowledgments

Thanks to Will Steeds and Laura Ward at Elephant Book Company, and Kevin Stevens at Imagine Books, for the chance to build this little monument to writers. Many thanks also to Robert Littleford for his fantastic illustrations, to Paul Palmer-Edwards for his crisp design, and to Andrew Lowe for guiding the book through the process. This book is dedicated to Annie, Sascha, and Eli (with thanks to Patsey for lending us her retreat and putting up with us), and to my mother and father, for everything.